time to grow
BOOK 3

CHRISTINE MEADEN

Angel Press

First published by Angel Press
P.O. Box 60, Chichester, West Sussex PO20 8RA
in 1985

Cover photograph by Pictor

British Library Cataloguing in Publication Data

Meaden, Christine
Time to Grow, Book 3
1. Schools — Great Britain — Prayers
2. Schools — Great Britain — Exercises and recreations
I. Title
377'.1   BV283.S3

ISBN 0 947785 06 X

Printed in England by
Whitstable Litho Limited
and produced by
Arachne Marketing Services

CONTENTS

CONTENTS *continued*

ACKNOWLEDGEMENTS

The author would like to thank the following for permission to reprint extracts from their works. If there are any omissions, she would be pleased to make an acknowledgement in any further reprint.

A Japanese translation of Psalm 23 by Toki Miyashino, *British Weekly,* 5th September, 1958; "Give us Love, Lord," Gillian Catu, by permission of E.H. Goddard; *Parish Prayers,* by Frank Colquhoun by permission of Hodder & Stoughton Ltd.; *Prayer for Prayer,* by John Eddison by permission of Henry E. Walter Ltd.; "A Job or an Adventure" from *Stories for the Junior Assembly* by permission of Blandford Press; "Bonfire Night" from *Stories Round the Year* and prayers from *Prayers to Use for 8's to 11's* by permission of the National Christian Education Council; The prayer beginning "God our Father ...." is from The Alternative Service Book 1980 and is reproduced by permission of the Central Board of Finance of the Church of England.

NEW PLACES, NEW FACES

Aim: *To show that barriers of culture and language can be overcome in a holiday setting.*

Aids: *Flippers and snorkel; a plate of spaghetti, fork and spoon.*

Presentation: Simon wasn't at all sure he wanted to go on holiday. His mum and dad were leafing through brochures about camping abroad. The camping part was alright; abroad was not. All the places sounded strange, and he didn't fancy not being able to buy sweets or fizzy lemonade because he didn't know the words.

Finally his parents made their choice and booked in to a campsite near the border of France and Italy, on a lake where there was water-skiing, boating and fishing. Simon dreamed about catching a big fish and frying it over a camp fire. But he was still worried about being lonely. What if he got lost, and couldn't even ask his way back to the tent?

When the time came to pack, Simon made sure his suitcase had plenty of biscuits, cola and crisps, just in case. He went to bed, but had trouble getting to sleep, wondering what the French and Italians would look like. The next day, the long journey began, first by car, then ferry, then a long, long drive. Sometimes Simon slept, sometimes he listened to story-tapes and sometimes he pestered his mum to play Twenty Questions. Once or twice, they stopped for petrol, and he heard people all around him chattering away, but not one word sounded familiar. His heart sank.

Finally, they turned off the main road into a narrower one, with trees and fields on either side; then soon after that onto a single lane gravel road. Ahead of them was the sign Lac Philippe. And beyond the entrance gate a large lake lay shining in the evening sun.

Putting up the tent always seemed to bring out the worst in his parents, Simon thought, although when it was up, it was a great place to sleep. His mum and dad had one big compartment; he had a smaller one, and they could zip themselves in at night to keep the insects out. After a supper of sausages and beans and rolls from the campsite shop, Simon had no trouble getting to sleep.

He was wakened next morning by a scurrying sound, and quietly, very quietly, he padded over to where it came from. Just by the front flap of the tent was a little hole with a tail disappearing into it. Simon opened the box of cornflakes and gently put a few round the hole. After a few minutes, a sniffing nose appeared, and one by one the cornflakes disappeared. Simon had made his first friend.

Down by the lake, he discovered a whole colony of frogs, and practised for hours until he could catch one.

He learned how to use a snorkel and flippers, and soon he felt just like a frog himself, jumping in and swimming under water.

On the second day, he saw a boy playing marbles by himself, and Simon went a bit closer to watch. Eventually the boy noticed him and said "Bonjour." By now, Simon knew that was French for "hello", and so he tried to say it back. Soon, the boy had shown Simon the rules of his game, and by pointing to each other, Simon learned that the boy's name was Guy (pronounced guee). They swam together that day, and Simon felt that this holiday was not so bad, especially when you only had to point in the shop to get fizzy lemonade.

After a few days, Simon and Guy were chattering away in a mixture of French and English, and so were their parents.

They all went to Italy together (the border was only a few miles away) and had huge white napkins round their necks while they are spaghetti bolognaise, winding it round a fork pressed onto a spoon (the presenter might demonstrate). They walked through the town and up to an old castle, which was cool and dark after the bright heat of the town. Simon and Guy pretended to defend the ramparts against invaders.

The days passed without really being counted, until suddenly, it was the last day. Simon packed all his souvenirs, his postcards, his collection of pebbles, a special marble from

Guy and a new hat he had bought in Italy with a green sun shade. He put lots of cornflakes out for his mouse, and felt very sad as he let go of the last frog he had caught.

From the back seat of the car, he waved goodbye to Guy and the lake. "Au revoir," he whispered softly.

Prayer:
For long summer days,
With holidays,
We thank you heavenly Father.

For river and sea,
Limbs running free,
We thank you heavenly Father.

For tents on the site,
Camp fires at night,
We thank you heavenly Father.

For games in the park,
Sleep after dark,
We thank you heavenly Father.

For far away places,
and meeting new faces,
We thank you heavenly Father.

For playing new games,
and visiting towns with new names,
We thank you heavenly Father.

From *Prayers to use with 8–11's*
with additional verses

Follow-up:
• *Ask the children to pretend they don't speak the same language. Ask them in pairs to mime actions to communicate e.g asking for a drink, inviting someone to play, showing the rules of a game, exchanging names.*
• *Make a list of food we eat, which originated in other countries, or is representative of other countries.*

HOLIDAY AT HOME

Aim: *To show that a holiday at home need not make children dissatisfied.*

Many of you have had exciting holidays, visiting new places, but it isn't always possible to go away for holidays. Sometimes it is just as exciting to stay at home. Today I am going to tell you a story of two children who did just that.

David and Susan were feeling rather sad, they were not able to go away for a holiday this year, because their mother was ill in hospital, waiting for their new baby to arrive, and their father was working, so Aunty Jean had come to stay for the summer holidays.

Susan and David lived in a small market town with a very ancient castle, and old twisty streets which led out onto the moors, where, deep under the hills, lay the remains of old tin mines, boarded up and long out of use.

After the first few days of playing at home, helping Aunty Jean 'keep house', and running errands, David and Susan began to get rather bored. They missed their mother, and although Dad took them to visit her every evening, they wished she would soon be home with their new baby brother or sister. Aunty Jean was 'alright', but she was getting rather old, and was tired of them 'getting under her feet' as she put it. After one particular day when it had rained non-stop, and the children had been squabbling, Aunty Jean found a story to tell them. It turned out to be rather a super story, for Aunty Jean had lived in the town all of her life, and knew a great deal of its history. This story was one of the legends that surrounded the great granite castle which stood on the hill, a tale of knights and ghosts, which thrilled David to bits, but sent shivers down Susan's spine!

Next day dawned bright and sunny. "What shall we do?" said Susan. "I know," said David, "let's go up to the castle." Susan suppressed a shiver. "It's okay, silly!" said her brother, "Ghosts only come out in the dark." Susan laughed, and the two children set off on the steep climb up the hill to the castle entrance.

There were many other people peering at the displays and costumes in the various rooms. "All tourists," said David. They saw Dukes and Duchesses in grand finery, soldiers in magnificent battle dress, rooms with beautiful furniture and pictures, and, the deep dark dungeons! As the children looked at the displays in the castle museum, they noticed a completely empty case, empty that is except for a notice saying: "Lord Stuart Trevelyn's C18 jewelled sword and sheath – stolen 1933 – as yet unrecovered, believed stolen locally." Then there followed a detailed description of the sword, and a photograph. "What a shame it's missing," said Susan. "Yes," said her brother, "H'm, believed stolen locally, that's interesting."

The children finished their tour and not having seen a ghost, much to Susan's relief! they tramped home for tea, and told Aunty Jean and their father what they had seen.

A few days later the children cycled out to the moors for a picnic. After a long ride, they sat down to eat their lunch. Looking around, David could see a 'hump' in the distance, with something on the top glittering in the sunlight. "What's that over there?" asked Susan. "Let's go and see," said David, jumping up. "Race you there." The children arrived panting at the 'hump', which turned out to be the remains of a disused tin mine. Someone or something had dislodged the boarding and the sunlight was glinting onto a plaque placed high on the wall. "Let's explore," said David. "It's too dark," said his sister. "Oh, come on, don't be a baby; no ghosts here," replied David teasingly.

Together, the two children edged their way along the old mine shaft, fingering their way along the cold, clammy walls. "Ouch!" said David suddenly. "What's wrong?" said Susan. "It's my hand, it hit something very sharp." "It's okay, I can get hold of it now," David said. "It's something long and lumpy." Very carefully he lifted down a long, thin object covered in old sacking. "Let me see," said Susan. "Wait a minute; let's get over to the light," said her brother, as he lifted his 'prize' over to where the sunlight was creeping in. "Whatever can it be?" Susan wondered. David carefully unwound the sacking, and there, tarnished with damp and old age, lay a beautiful bejewelled sword. "It's the sword from the museum," exclaimed the two children together.

"Let's take it back to the castle right now," said David. So rather shakily, David rode his bicycle back over the bumpy path, with the splendid sword, still wrapped in its damp sacking, precariously perched over the handlebars. Susan rode excitedly in front of her brother, thinking "Have we really found the lost sword?"

Eventually, very tired, the children climbed up the hill to the castle. When they told their story to the gatekeeper, they were taken to see Mr Simmonds, the curator of the museum. He was amazed and overjoyed at the children's find, and carefully examined the sword, comparing it to the original photograph.

"You really have found Lord Trevelyn's sword," he said at last, "the most valuable piece that the museum possesses. I think Castleford will be mighty proud of our young treasure hunters!"

The next few days were extremely busy for David and Susan. They were asked to attend a presentation where Mr Simmonds told everyone how they had found Lord Trevelyn's long-lost sword. Each of them was given a gold medallion as a memento of their historic find, and their photographs appeared in the local newspapers. They were heroes for the rest of the holidays!

However, their greatest surprise was yet to come, for one morning Dad woke them up with the news that they now had a new brother AND sister. "Twins!" said the children. "Smashing!" "This really has been a super holiday after all," said Susan.

Prayer: Father of all, we thank you for holidays at home, for time to explore our surroundings and discover more about your beautiful world — how the sunlight glints on the wet roads, the delicate pattern of a spider's web and beautiful rainbows.

We thank you too for time to be with our families, to enjoy each other's company, and be together. Just as David and

Susan enjoyed their holiday at home, each one of us gives you thanks now for the many things we have enjoyed during our holidays.

Follow-up:
- *Take a map of your village, town or neighbourhood, and mark on all the places where you might spend holiday time, e.g. the swimming pool, playing fields, adventure playground and museums.*
- *Plan a tour of your area for someone from another place.*
- *Make a chart of children's free-time activities. Encourage those who do little to consider a craft or hobby. Have library books available to stimulate interest.*

THE ELEPHANT AND THE RAT

Accepting Differences

Aim: *To help children accept differences in others, without trying to boss or bully each other.*

Aids: *A large and a small swimsuit.*

Presentation: Here is a story about the elephant and the rat. One very hot day in the jungle, the elephant heaved himself to his feet and thought, "I'd feel much cooler after a dip in the pool below the waterfall." Although it made him feel even hotter to get there, once he waded in right up to his belly, he began to cool off. He filled his trunk with water and showered his steamy back. Then he trumpeted for joy and splashed with his legs, flapping his ears, too. And he sat down.

As he was enjoying his dip, a rat came along and watched him for a few minutes. Then he said, "I want you to get out of that pool."

"I won't," said the elephant. "Why should I? I'm having a lovely time and I'm not ready to come out yet."

"I insist you get out this minute," said the rat, waving his paws about and twitching his whiskers.

"Why?" asked the elephant.

"I shall tell you that only when you are out of that pool," replied the rat.

"Then I won't get out," snapped back the elephant.

But eventually he gave in, and ponderously waded towards the shore, setting up huge waves in his wake.

"Now then," he said, towering over the rat, "why did you want me out of the pool?"

"To check if you were wearing my swimsuit," said the rat.

Now doesn't that seem ridiculous, that the rat ever thought the elephant could get into his swimsuit? But let's think about it a minute. Have you ever come up to two other children playing a game and tried to get them to play what you wanted to play? Have you ever tried to persuade someone to go home the way you wanted to go?

Very often, we try to push and pull other people to do what we want, when we want to, even though they are not very willing. Part of having friends is to ask what others would like to do, not always insisting on our own way. Would an elephant's swimsuit fit you?

Prayer: Dear God, you have made each one of us different from each other, and you love us for the unique person each of us is. Help us to recognise the differences in each other, and to make room for wishes and points of view different from our own. Keep us from bossing and bullying and give us a spirit of sharing. Amen.

Follow-up:
● *Ask the children to work in pairs and compile a list of all the differences between each other.*
● *Look at the twelve men Jesus chose to be his special friends. Examine the differences between them.*
● *Introduce the theme of racial differences, and try to develop understanding where there may be prejudice.*

WELCOME

Aim: *To deal with some fears and anxieties commonly felt by pupils arriving at a new school for the first time.*

Aids: *New items of school uniform.*

Presentation:

Bryan's first day

Zring! Zringgg! Zrinnggg!! went the alarm clock and Bryan woke up with a jump. Gosh was it a quarter past seven already? He leapt out of bed and saw his new school uniform hanging over the chair. Full of excitement, for today was his first day at Gatesford Middle School, Bryan got dressed and ran downstairs to eat his breakfast. His baby sister gurgled at him and he felt very grown up.

Today he was going to travel on the school bus which would pick him up by the corner shop. Having said "Goodbye" to Mum and baby sister (Dad had already gone to work) Bryan walked down the street swinging his new shoebag. As he got nearer to the corner his tummy began to rumble and he felt very nervous. Suddenly breakfast didn't feel quite so good! "Do I really want to go to school today?" he asked himself.

Just then his friend Graham came around the corner and Bryan began to feel better. Together they jumped onto the bus. "Have your bus passes ready lads," called the driver. Bryan felt in his jacket pocket — it wasn't there! It wasn't in any of his other pockets either. All the other children began to look at him and Bryan began to panic, "Would he be thrown off the bus?" he thought. "Come on lad," said the driver, "You can't have lost it on your first day now. Turn out your bags and have a really good look." Bryan started searching through his satchel while Graham shook out his shoe bag. "Here it is," he cried, "tucked inside your plimsol!" Bryan gratefully took the ticket and showed it to the driver "Must have been my little sister." he said. Having packed everything back into the bags, the boys found a seat, Bryan feeling very embarrassed.

Soon they reached Gatesford Middle School, and getting off the bus, they saw a packed playground; children seemed to be everywhere! Some were chasing each other around; some were collecting conkers from under the trees; a group of girls were playing a skipping game; and some older boys were playing football.

Bryan and Graham looked anxiously around, and then they spotted a group of friends from their old school, all looking very new and talking to the teacher on duty. "Come over here," they cried, and soon Bryan and Graham found themselves swapping holiday stories and meeting some new friends. When the whistle blew, the teacher showed them where to line up and they all went into Assembly together.

Soon they were sorted out into their new classes and Bryan found that he was split up from Graham. He was on his own again! He began to feel lonely and a bit lost. Then his new teacher, Mr James called out their names and told them where to sit. Bryan found that he was sitting next to a boy called Simon.

Mr James talked to his new class and told them about the school: he explained the school rules and told them that they would be learning about new subjects, and there would be many new things to do — football, and cricket teams, chess and gym clubs, an orchestra and even a computer club. Bryan and Simon decided that they might join the cycling proficiency class, and Bryan thought that he might like to learn to play the guitar. "Of course," said Mr James, "I expect you to try your very best with all your work as well." "Oh dear," thought Bryan, "that means being tidy and getting my spellings right!"

The bell went for break and the class ran out onto the playground. Bryan and Simon made some more friends as they all played together. After break they had some English to do, and at lunch time the top class came to collect them for lunch. The canteen seemed very large to Bryan. Still, lunch was sausages and baked beans, which was one of his favourites, and the older children were very friendly and helpful.

During the afternoon all the new children went to House meetings, where they were told that the school was divided up into five Houses, and House points were given for games and work, (and also taken away sometimes). Bryan was in St Christopher's House. He was beginning to feel part of the new school family already. The afternoon passed quickly, and Bryan met new teachers for Music and RE, as well as having a History lesson with Mr James.

Finally the last bell rang, and, laden with books for his first 'homework', Bryan made his way out to wait for the bus. He met Graham again, and found that several of his new friends were on the same bus, so there was plenty to talk about on the way home.

Mum and Dad were anxious to here about his first day at his new school, and in telling them about all that had happened, Bryan began to feel as if he'd been there for years, instead of just one day. After a very talkative tea Bryan settled down to writing a story about William the Concquror, bringing his ships across the sea to invade Saxon England. "How do you spell Conqueror?" he wondered.

Prayer: Dear Lord, may our school be a welcoming place. Make us aware of each other's needs, and give us a spirit of helpfulness. Give us courage to ask for help when we need it.

Follow-up:
● *Begin a growth chart for each child, to be measured monthly throughout the year. Talk about signs of growing, physically and mentally.*
● *Make a skills survey of the class and illustrate it. Hobbies, sports, music and games should all be included, as well as more intangible skills such as helpfulness, and following instructions.*

RAINY DAY OUTING

Aim: *To show that it is often our attitude to circumstances that makes them good or bad, pleasant or disagreeable.*

Aids: *A raincoat, wellies and umbrella.*

Presentation: Many of you look forward to school outings long before they happen; and some of you are so excited the night before that you have difficulty getting to sleep. The person who looks forward longest, and sleeps worst the night before is the teacher! She's the one who has to make the booking, hire the coach, send home notices and make sure no-one gets left behind.

Mrs Thompson was watching the evening news. At least, she was waiting for the weather forecast. "We're taking fifty pupils to the Wildfowl Refuge tomorrow," she told her husband, "and I do hope it will be fine."

Mr Thompson grunted back, "You can never be sure this time of year."

"You can never be sure *any* time of the year in Britain," said Mrs Thompson. "I have reminded the children to bring raingear. And no glass bottles," she added as she mentally checked through the instructions she had put on the board that afternoon.

On came the weather forecast, with a big low pressure area heading straight for them. "Showery tomorrow," said the announcer, "with some heavy rain in places, but some sunny patches, too."

"Well, isn't that helpful," said Mrs Thompson. "We're going to have everything." And she stomped off to bed, but not to sleep. "Have I got the first aid kit ready? Will the parent helpers remember to turn up? And where is my umbrella?" Finally she dropped off to sleep, dreaming of the class floating in Noah's Ark on the flood.

The next day dawned calm and clear, except for a thin grey line on the horizon. "Perhaps we'll be lucky after all," Mrs

Thompson muttered to herself as she rushed out of the door, with her sandwich lunch under her arm.

Carefully, she sorted the children into friendly groups, each with a parent helper in charge. She kept two of the most boisterous with her. All the pocket money was collected and recorded, and after one packed lunch was inspected for leakage, everyone headed for the waiting coach in their groups.

By the time the coach arrived at the Wildfowl Refuge, the sky was clouding over. They all trooped into the theatre first, for a presentation by one of the bird wardens. She had big cardboard duck heads to try on for imitating eider ducks, and lots of slides showing the differences between ducks, swans and geese.

There were no windows in the theatre, so when the children came out into the reception area, they were disappointed to see rain falling in the ponds. "Well," said Mrs Thompson, "we must make the best of it. Let's have lunch and hope it stops so that we can walk round outside before we go."

Lunch improved everyone's spirits, especially crisps and chocolate biscuits, which were not on the school dinner menu. By the time the last wrappers were hurled into bins, the classes were raring to go.

"Please, Mrs Thompson," said Edward, "we've all got anoraks. Please, let us go out and feed the ducks."

Mrs Thompson looked at the steady drizzle. "Oh well," she sighed, "we're only two hours away from dry clothes. Very well. Let's go and watch the ducks." The parent helpers rounded up their groups with resigned expressions. They didn't want to get wet.

When they reached the first pond, and found a clearing in the reeds, there were ducks in action everywhere. Black and white eider ducks were bobbing under and up, showering themselves. Small grey and brown pochards disappeared altogether, then popped up much further away. Some of the children counted to see how long they stayed under. Sarah timed a full minute for her duck. A group of shell duck with handsome brown markings waddled onto the shore and quacked at the children, wanting food. Michael and Cathy went very slowly and quietly near the ducks and crouched down holding out flat hands with grain. The bravest ducks came right up and fed out of their hands.

All the ducks were in their bright mating plumage, and didn't mind the rain one bit. The oil in their feathers kept them from getting cold and wet. The children were too busy and interested looking for nests and young to mind the rain either. They scampered from pond to pond, finding rare South American ducks sharing their quarters with humble moorhens.

Mrs Thompson looked at her watch and said, "Goodness. It's time to get back to the coach. Hurry, now children, but don't run and mind the cars in the car park."

On the way back, all the windows were steamed up from wet jackets, but nobody minded. And Stephen felt his pocket to make sure his half-full bag of grain was still there. He had saved some for the ducks on his village pond.

Prayer: Dear God, we thank you for all weathers, for sunshine, wind and rain. We pray for all places where there is danger of too much; where there is desert, hurricane or flood. Make us to be eager to help. May we always respect your creatures and to learn about them, that we may ensure that there is room and food for all of them. Amen.

Follow-up:
● *Take a rain survey, measuring the quantity over a month and plotting it on a graph.*
● *Make a class poem, each child contributing a line about rain: its sight, sounds, smells and effects.*
● *Find out the differences between ducks, geese and swans.*

FRIENDSHIP

Aim: *To establish qualities of friendship: trust, love, sharing.*

Aids: *On a board in large letters, these words: TRUST, LOVE, SHARE.*

Presentation:
The Happy Prince

High above the city (of Copenhagen) on a tall column, stood the statue of the Happy Prince. He was gilded all over with fine gold, for eyes he had two bright sapphires, and a large red ruby glowed on his sword-hilt. All the townspeople loved him for he smiled at them as they went about their daily journeys.

One night a little swallow flew over the city. His friends had gone away to Egypt six weeks before, but he had stayed behind, for he was in love with a most beautiful river reed. Sadly in the autumn he grew tired of his love and flew away.

All day long he flew, and at night time he arrived at the city. "Where shall I stay?" he said. "I hope the town has made preparations for me." Then he saw the statue on the tall column. "I will put up there," he cried, "it is a fine position, with plenty of fresh air." So he perched between the feet of the Happy Prince. As he sat there he suddenly felt a large drop of water falling on him, then another and another. "How curious," he thought, "It is not raining." He looked up and what did he see? The eyes of the Happy Prince were filled with tears, and tears were running down his golden cheeks. His face was so beautiful in the moonlight that the little swallow was filled with pity.

"Who are you?" he asked, and the statue replied, "I am the Happy Prince.

"Why are you weeping then?" asked the swallow. "You have quite drenched me."

"When I was alive and had a human heart," answered the

statue, "I did not know what tears were, for I had such a happy life, full of much pleasure and beauty. Now that I am dead they have set me up here so high that I can see all the ugliness and misery of my city.

Far away," continued the statue, "in a little street there is a poor house. One of the windows is open, and through it I can see a woman seated at a table. Her face is thin and worn, and she has coarse red hands, all pricked by the needle, for she is a seamstress. In a bed in a corner of the room her little boy is lying ill. He has a fever, and is asking for oranges. His mother has nothing to give him but river water, so he is crying. Swallow, swallow, little swallow, will you not bring her the ruby out of my sword hilt? My feet are fastened to this pedestal and I cannot move."

"I am expected in Egypt," said the swallow. "My friends are lying up and down the Nile, and talking to the large lotus flowers."

"Swallow, swallow, little swallow," said the Prince, "will you not stay with me for one night, and be my messanger? The boy is so thirsty, and the mother so sad."

"I don't think I like little boys," said the swallow. But the Happy Prince looked so sad that the little swallow was sorry. "It is very cold here," he said, "but I will stay with you for one night, and be your messenger."

"Thank you little swallow," said the Prince. So the swallow plucked out the great ruby from the Prince's sword, and flew away with it in his beak over the town. He passed by the cathedral tower, over the river and the ghetto and at last he came to the poor house and looked in. The boy was tossing feverishly on his bed, and his mother had fallen asleep, she was so tired. In he hopped, and laid the great ruby on the table beside the woman's thimble. Then he flew gently round the bed, fanning the boy's forehead with his wings. "How cool I feel," said the boy. "I must be getting better," and he sank into a delicious slumber.

Then the swallow flew back to the Happy Prince and told him what he had done. "It is curious," he remarked, "but I feel quite warm now although it is so cold."

"That is because you have done a good act," said the Prince. And the little swallow began to think, and then he fell asleep. Thinking always made him sleepy.

Next day the little swallow flew around the city and when the moon rose he flew back to the Happy Prince. "Have you any commissions for Egypt?" he cried. "I am just starting."

"Swallow, swallow, my little swallow," said the Prince. "Will you not stay with me one night longer?"

"I am wanted in Egypt," said the swallow. "Tomorrow my friends will fly up to the second cataract."

"Swallow, swallow, little swallow," said the Prince, "far away across the city I see a young man in a garret. He is trying to finish a play for the Director of the Theatre, but he is too cold to write any more. There is no fire in the grate and hunger has made him faint."

"I will wait with you one night longer," said the swallow, who really had a good heart. "Shall I take him another ruby?"

"Alas! I have no ruby now," said the Prince: "my eyes are all that I have left, pluck out one of them and take it to him. He will sell it to the jeweller, and buy firewood, and finish his play."

"Dear Prince," said the swallow, "I cannot do that." And he began to weep.

"Swallow, swallow, little swallow," said the Prince, "do as I command you." So the swallow plucked out the Prince's eye and flew away to the student's garret. It was easy enough to get in, as there was a hole in the roof. The young man had his head buried in his hands, so did not hear the flutter of the bird's wings, and when he looked up he found the beautiful sapphire.

"I am beginning to be appreciated," he cried, "Now I can finish my play." And he looked quite happy.

Next evening the little swallow flew back to the Happy Prince. "I am come to bid you goodbye," he cried.

"Swallow, swallow, little swallow," cried the Prince, "will you not stay with me one night longer?"

"It is winter," answered the swallow," and the chill wind will soon be here. Dear Prince, I must leave you, but I will never forget you, and next spring I will bring you back two beautiful jewels in place of those you have given away."

"In the square below," said the Happy Prince, "there stands a little match girl. She has let her matches fall in the gutter, and they are all spoiled. Her father will beat her if she does not bring home some money, and she is crying. She has no shoes or stockings and her head is bare. Pluck out my other eye, and give it to her, and her father will not beat her."

"I will stay with you one night longer," said the swallow, "but I cannot pluck out your eye. You would be quite blind then."

"Swallow, swallow, little swallow, do as I command you," said the Prince. So he plucked out the Prince's other eye, and darted down with it. He swooped past the match girl and slipped the jewel into her hand. "What a lovely bit of glass!" cried the little girl; and she ran home laughing.

Then the swallow went back to the Prince, "You are blind now," he said, "so I will stay with you always."

"No, little swallow," said the poor prince, "you must go away to Egypt." "I will stay with you always," said the swallow, and he slept at the Prince's feet.

The poor little swallow grew colder and colder, but he would not leave the Prince; he loved him too well. He picked up crumbs outside the baker's door when the baker was not looking, and tried to keep himself warm by flapping his wings. But at last he knew that he was going to die. He had just enough strength to fly up to the Prince's shoulder once more. "Goodbye dear Prince!" he murmured, "will you let me kiss your hand?" "I am glad that you are going to Egypt at last, little swallow" said the Prince. "It is not to Egypt that I am going," said the swallow, I am going to the House of Death. Death is the brother of sleep is he not?" And he kissed the Prince and fell down dead at his feet. At that moment a curious crack sounded inside the statue, as if something had broken; the leaden heart had snapped in two.

The dead bird was thrown onto the dust heap in the town, and the statue of the Happy Prince was pulled down, for without his jewels he was no longer beautiful.

In heaven God said to one of his angels "Bring me the two

23

most precious things in the city," and the angel brought Him the leaden heart and the dead bird. "You have rightly chosen," said God, "for in my garden of Paradise this little bird shall sing for evermore, and in my city of gold the Happy Prince shall praise me."

Adapted from the story by Oscar Wilde

Prayer:

> Dear God, thank you for our friends,
> Friends we can trust,
> Friends who make us feel happy
> and friends who help us.
> Help us always to be good friends, never to leave anyone out in the cold, when we could offer friendship.
> Help us to share our sorrows and our happy times, and to love each other as you love us.
>
> Amen

Follow-up:
- *A friendship questionnaire, e.g:*
  1. *Who would you choose to sit next to? Why?*
  2. *Who would you like to be in a netball/football team with?*
  3. *Who would you like to go on your holidays with? Why?*
  4. *Who would you share your most precious possession with? Why?*
  5. *What would you do if you knew your best friend was doing something wrong?*
  6. *What would you do if he/she were locked in the classroom?*

DAVID AND JONATHAN : TRUST AND LOVE

Aim: *To develop and strengthen friendships already formed.*

Presentation: We all need our friends; can you think of any special times when you really need to have a friend? (to celebrate, a special game, when in trouble, mending a bike, etc.).

Here is a story about a friend in need:

You remember the story of how David killed the Philistine giant Goliath? Well, this is another story about David. He had grown up to become a strong soldier in the Israelite army, and he had become a special friend of the king's son, Jonathan, even though Jonathan was the son of the king and he only a poor shepherd boy.

The country was still at war with the Philistines; food was short and went mostly to the soldiers. Many homes had been destroyed and soldiers killed, but David had become very successful, and had killed tens of thousands of Philistines in battle. This had made King Saul extremely jealous of David and he plotted to kill him, but Jonathan decided because David was his best friend, that he would warn him. So after telling David of his plan, Jonathan and one of his servants went out to some fields where he often practised shooting arrows.

David was hiding in the field behind some boulders. He saw Jonathan coming – could he really rely on him he wondered? Of course he could, for they had always been friends, in lots of difficult times! This time though, David's life depended on Jonathan's true friendship.

"Run and find the arrows," Jonathan said to his servant, and as the boy ran ahead he began to shoot his arrows at a target some way away. David watched carefully and listened as he heard Jonathan say "Look, the arrows are in front of you, hurry up, run and get them for me. There's no time to lose." David's heart sank, for this was the sign that Saul still wanted to kill him, and he must escape quickly if he was to stay alive.

The servant boy found the arrows in the long grass, and Jonathan sent him back to the palace. Now David could come out of hiding. He bowed three times to Jonathan (for he was a prince remember), and then both lads feeling very unhappy indeed, said their goodbyes. Both knew that they might never see each other again. As they hugged each other Jonathan said, "Go in safety, for we will always be true friends." As he ran, David realised what a really good friend Jonathan had been, for he knew that Saul would be very angry with his son for warning David. Jonathan was the best friend he could ever have.

Prayer: Dear Lord Jesus, we remember today how Jonathan helped David when he was in trouble, help us to trust each other in friendship, and make us ready always to help our friends, especially when they really need us to be kind and helpful to them.

Thank you for giving us many opportunities to show each other what being a friend really means, and may we remember that You are always our true Friend. Amen.

Follow-up:
- *Portraits of best friends in words and/or art.*
- *Play a trust game, where a child is blindfolded and led over an obstacle course by a friend.*

SHARING A DAY'S FISHING

Aim: *To develop a sense of responsibility for one's friend.*

Aids: *A fishing rod.*

Presentation: Has anyone got a penfriend? What do you write to each other about? Why do we have penfriends?

Sometimes we are lucky enough to meet and make friends with people who come to our country from another country, either on holiday, or to live. Our story is about just that:

Jim's family had just moved to a new house in a new town. Dad, as a Doctor had a job in a big hospital. Jim was just starting at a new school. He missed his old friends, but soon became busy in helping to redecorate his room in the new house.

One day he was playing football in the garden, when next door he saw a boy playing with an aeroplane. Jim said, "Hello. What's your name?" and he and Jindra began talking about themselves. Jindra was going to the same school, and was in the same class as Jim was to be. They soon became close friends and played together at weekends. Jindra's father was also a doctor. Both of the boys enjoyed fishing, so they would often spend some time together down by the river; sometimes they caught a fish!

Jindra knew of a good spot for fishing. One summer day the boys decided to take a picnic and spend the day fishing by the river. They cast their lines and during the morning managed to catch a few small fish. After their picnic they agreed to move up the river. This was to a more dangerous spot where the river flowed faster. They set their lines as before then decided to wander off and explore. Clambering about over the slippery rocks they hunted frogs, admired iridescent dragon-flies, and found some freshwater shrimp.

After a while they returned to their lines and settled down by the river bank. Suddenly Jim's line twitched — he had a bite! Pulling in his line was very hard work; it must be something big! Just as he thought he'd nearly won, Jim's foot slipped on the edge of the bank, and in he fell.

The river was running high, dragging Jim downstream. He was very scared. Jindra tried to stretch out his fishing rod, but Jim was too far out. As Jindra ran along the bank beside his friend, he spied a longer pole, and quickly shoved it out in front of Jim, who caught hold of it. Carefully Jindra pulled Jim to the shore.

Both of the boys, very wet and shaken, went home to explain their escapade to their parents. They had had enough fishing for one day. Jim was always very grateful to his friend Jindra, and the two boys remained firm friends for the rest of their lives.

Prayer: Father, we thank you for our friends — those we make at school and at home. We thank you for all they do to make us happy, and that we can talk with them, laugh and play with them. Help us never to lose a good friend by being unkind or untruthful, and to remember how good you are to your friends, even when they hurt you and sadden you by what they say and do.   Amen.

Follow-up:
● *An opportunity to discuss water safety and rescue, e.g NEVER jump in to save another person or animal unless you are a qualified life-saver. Look for an object to reach out with: rope, broom handle, branch. Get help from the nearest adult.*
● *Make a survey of activities that are more fun with a friend, and draw out elements of sharing.*

WE NEED EACH OTHER

Aim: *To gain an understanding of the different types of harvest, of the products, human effort and interdependence involved in its production.*

Aids: *Packet of tea, bunch of bananas.*

Presentation: Hold up a packet of tea. Does anyone know where this comes from? Ask the children what else they have eaten for their breakfast and if they know where the articles are grown etc. Hold up a large bunch of big, ripe bananas. How many people and jobs are involved in getting these bananas to our tables?

Bananas are tropical plants grown only in hot countries such as the Canary Islands, Jamaica and the Windward Isles.

Bananas are grown on plantations, the roots are planted and the shoots grow quickly into an underground stem, which is very thick. The shoot grows to a height of six to twenty-five feet. It takes a year before the plant is ready to produce any fruit. When this happens the stalk (the banana) grows from a purple bud. Growing towards the sun, clusters of bananas are called a 'hand'. The bananas are picked when they are still green and unripe using a long pole and a knife called a 'Machete'. The cut 'hands' of bananas are then taken to cool storage sheds, and then to the docks where they are loaded onto ships for export. When they arrive in Britain they are unloaded and taken to warm ripening rooms, where they stay until they turn a golden yellow colour and are ready to be boxed and taken by lorry to shops and supermarkets.

Have eight children dressed to represent the following — mother, shop assistant, lorry driver, wholesaler, docker, docker in Jamaica, picker, grower, each with their particular verse on card.

Poem

I am the mother who shops for you all,
who chooses the bananas I see on the stall.

I am the grocer who works hard every day,
to sell the bananas so ripe on display.

I am the lorry driver, in my lorry all day,
bringing the fruit along the great motorways.

I am the buyer, I inspect all I see,
to make sure all is good, for you, and for me.

I am the docker who unloads all the crates,
of bananas and oranges, apples and dates.

I am the docker who works hard in the sun,
to load the bananas, their journey begun.

I am the picker working hard with my hands,
to gather the bananas from far foreign lands.

I am the grower who plants all the trees,
and tends them with care, so from pests they are free.

We work all together, but we work not alone,
for it is God who sends the rain and warm sun,
to grow fine big bananas, so yellow and ripe,
for you to enjoy when your day's work is done.

Prayer: God our Father, you have given us the gift of life,
Response: We thank you.
You have given us all the fruits of the earth,
Response:
For bananas, pineapple, oranges from far away,
Response:

For apples, pears, plums and cherries from our
country,

Response:

For bread, buns and cakes, made with loving care,

Response:

For all your gifts to us,

Response:
Amen.

Follow-up:

- *Recipe for Simple Banana Bread*

3 large ripe bananas	*1 tsp. salt*
2 eggs lightly beaten	*1 tsp. bicarb.*
150 g sugar	*150 g chopped nuts*
300 g flour	*½ tsp. ground cinnamon or ginger*

*Crush bananas, sprinkle with spice. Add eggs and sugar. Mix.
Add flour, salt and bicarb. Mix all well and put into a greased
pan. Bake in a moderate oven for about one hour.*

- *Look at packets of rice, cocoa, tins of fruit and mark on a
world map where each comes from. Put tacks in, and thread to
our own country.*

WHAT IS PRAYER?

Aim: *To encourage children to understand that prayer is our response to the continual presence of God.*

Aids: *OHP or shadow screen   — praying hands*
                                           — a figure at prayer.

Presentation: Ask the children what activity the aids illustrate. You could mime the posture of prayer as an alternative.

What is prayer? Prayer is talking and listening to God. Sometimes it is difficult to imagine that God is everywhere. Once, there was a small fish in the ocean, who asked an older fish, "Where is the ocean? I really want to swim there." The older fish replied, "You are already swimming in it." But the little fish was very disappointed at this answer. "Oh," he replied, "this is only water. I want to swim in the big ocean." And he wiggled his tail and swam off in search of the ocean.

Often we are looking for God, when he is already close to us. We only have to realise this.

Why do we pray? When we receive a gift, we want to say thank you. God gives us the gifts of life, of every new day, of the love of family and friends. (Children may add further examples.) Sometimes we need help and we can ask God for courage to do the right thing, for strength to carry through a task we find difficult, for guidance to make the right choices. Here is a story of someone who asked for help:

Answered Prayer

The crew of a Flying Fortress had to take to their life-rafts after being forced down at sea while on a routine mission en route to Australia. Eight of the nine crewmen were greatly worried. The ninth, Sergeant Hernandez, began to pray. Shortly thereafter, he startled the rest by announcing that help was on the way. He continued to pray. At the end of the second day they were rescued by native Australian fishermen near a lonely coral reef. These natives had been several hundred miles from the mainland in their outrigger canoes, and had turned homeward with their catch, when a 'strange urge came over them'. Something impelled them to alter their course and stear for the worthless, uninhabited little coral island where the airmen had drifted.

When do we pray? (Children may give suggestions.) Point out that at special times, such as assembly or church services people pray together. We should pray every day. Just as we meet our friends at school daily, we should make time for God too. Whenever we feel like it, we can call to mind God's constant presence. He has said in the Bible that he is closer to us than the veins in our neck. That is very close.

Prayer: (1) What is prayer, God?
It's talking to you —
    that's easy to do.
It's listening to you —
    that's harder.

How shall we hear you?
You won't speak in a loud, booming voice.
To listen we must be quiet,
    keep still,
    stop thinking our busy thoughts.

And then, gradually.
    we may find that we know
    what you want us to do,
    how you want us to live.

Gradually
we may realise you are there.
Help us to talk to you
Help us to *listen.*

Prayer: (2)   'Lord, teach us how to pray.'
Your disciples said it long ago.
We say it today.

'Don't show off when you pray,' you said.
'Pray in your own room by yourself.'
Help us to make a habit of talking to you
    and talking to God
    each day
    quietly
    on our own.

'Don't use a lot of words,' you said.
'Don't keep on and on.''
Help us to remember to keep our prayers
    short
    and simple.

'All you need to do is ask,' you said.
Help us to remember
    that God will give us good things,
    because He is our Father who loves us.

Follow-up:
● *Explore ways people have aids to prayer: rosary, prayer shawl, prayer mat, special pictures and verses from the Bible.*
● *Try different postures: kneeling, lying flat on one's stomach, standing with hands in front, palms upward, sitting. Ask children which they prefer, and suggest that our bodies can pray, as well as our lips. A short period of silence may be helpful, to listen to God.*

HOW DO WE PRAY?

Aim: *To show that God responds to our prayer.*

Aids: *Flannel/magnetic board and large cut out letters:*
A — Adoration of God, praise, creator, etc.
C — Confession, telling God that we're sorry.
T— Thanksgiving, thanking God for all his gifts to us.
S — Supplication, supplying help, asking for others.
Explain that ACTS = action in daily life.

Reading:

Isaiah's call to be a prophet — Isaiah 6

Isaiah was a priest in the temple in Jerusalem. He came from a family of priests, for his father had been a priest before him. It was part of the rules of the temple that each priest took it in turn to enter the holiest part of the temple, where only the very special and important priests were allowed. This was the part of the temple where God was felt to be closest. Only very occasionally was each priest allowed to go there. Today it was the turn of Isaiah, and while he was in the Holiest of Holies performing certain ceremonies and praying to God, he became aware of a great light surrounding him. Isaiah hid his eyes from what was happening. He had a strange vision that there he saw the Lord God sitting high on his throne, filling the whole temple with a glorious light. Surrounding him were magnificent and strange creatures, each with six wings. Isaiah was stunned: each creature covered its face with two wings, its body with two, and used two wings for flying. As they flew around the sanctuary, these creatures called,

> Holy, Holy, Holy
> The Lord Almighty is HOLY
> His glory fills the world!

Isaiah was astounded and filled with an intense awareness of the holiness of God, and of his own great sinfulness. But yet,

God had chosen this moment to reveal himself to him, a mere priest. What did this mean? Was this a special sign? What must he do?

As he stood there, hardly daring to raise his eyes, one of the creatures flew down to him, carrying a hot coal from the altar. He touched Isaiah's lips with it and said, "This has made your lips pure and now all your guilt has gone. You are forgiven." As if coming out of a strange and wonderful dream, Isaiah heard God's voice saying, "Whom shall I send? Who will be my messenger?" Immediately Isaiah knew what he must do: "I will go. I will give you message to your people," he said.

So, for many years to come, that is just what Isaiah did. He became a prophet of God to the Israelites, telling them much about God, of his love for them, and, of his holiness.

Prayer: Dear God, we love and adore you, we thank you for loving each one of us, and giving us your world in which to live. We are sorry for the times when we are unkind and hurtful, or selfish towards one another, please help us to think of others first before we speak or act.

We thank you Lord, for all the things which make us happy, (family, friends, playing and working together) and we ask you to bless anyone who is feeling sad or lonely today. Help us all to love each other as you love us.   Amen.

Follow-up:
● *Make a stained glass (grease proof or other translucent paper with black card cut-out "lead").*
● *Discuss the way of life of Julian of Norwich.*

Lady Julian was born during the fourteenth century, in 1342 in the city of Corwich (find on map). She spent much of her adult life in a small cell two steps beneath the medieval church of St Peter and St Julian. Her cell had two windows, one of which looked out into the church so that she could receive Holy Communion, and the other looked out into the garden, where many people came to talk to her and to ask her for advice on their problems and help in praying. She was called an anchoress because she was 'anchored' in her cell, and she lived for many years in this way, writing, praying, reading and meditating. She also had many holy visions and a deep unshakeable faith, an assurance that we are each personally loved by God.

● *Explain what a vision is, an experience so real, so life-changing, that it is as though the recipient has seen it physically. We can only communicate through familiar senses, such as sight, sound and touch, and all great spiritual experiences can only be related in these terms.*

● *Ask the children to write prayers based on ACTS, and display them under that heading.*

Plan of the Temple

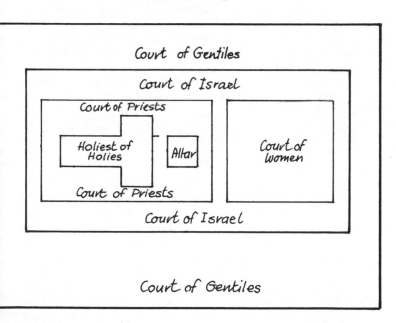

37

THE LORD'S PRAYER : WHO ARE YOU LORD?

Aim: *To show that God is a loving father.*

Presentation: Your name stands for you, your identity and character. It tells everyone who you are. Just the same with God who created us all. His name of Father stands for love, all the goodness and trust and care which we associate with our parents who love us. God our Father is the Father of all mankind. He is the head of a very special family. God our Father will go on loving us all the time, even when we do things that are wrong. He wants us to love and to trust him just as we do our human parents.

All our names have a special meaning for us, my name is me! Sometimes we have pet names or nicknames, these are often linked with what we look like or what we do, Shorty, Lanky, Speedy. Jesus had a special name for his Father too, he called Him Abba (Daddy).

God is Love, his name stands for Love, therefore we should use His name with respect and reverence. "Hallowed be thy name," means that God's name is to be used in a respectful and worshipping way, never carelessly. One person who did just this was Daniel when he was thrown to the lions.

Daniel

Daniel was one of the chief ministers in King Darius' government, he was a very busy man, overseeing the work of the farmers and merchants, seeing that they did not cheat the King or overprice their goods. Daniel was very honest, he respected and served his king well, and in return Darius valued Daniel and wished to promote him to become his Chief Governor.

Some of the other ministers grew jealous of Daniel and plotted against him, to put him out of the King's favour. They knew that they could not accuse Daniel of not doing his work properly, so they decided to attack him through his belief in God.

Having made their sinister plan, the ministers went to speak to the king, "King Darius, may your majesty live for ever. As your chief ministers we have a matter of state to put before you. It is our belief that to deepen the people's respect for you, you should issue a strict order, an order that is to be obeyed upon penalty of death." After talking with his ministers, the king signed and issued a proclamation which said, "I, Darius, King of the Medes and ruler over all, make an order that during the next thirty days, no one, man, woman, or child shall worship any god but myself, on pain of death by the lions."

When Daniel heard of the order he went to his room and continued praying to God three times a day, even though he realised what would happen to him. Sure enough a few days later Daniel was arrested and brought before the King, who had by this time realised that his ministers had tricked him. Unfortunately the order could not be broken.

Sadly he said, "Daniel, my trusted servant, you of all people have disobeyed my orders, orders which are laws of the Medes and the Persians and which cannot be changed. Now I have no choice but to punish you by throwing you into the lions pit; but you are a loyal servant to your God, do not fear for He will rescue you." Daniel was taken away by the guards and forced into the lion's pit, where the hungry lions roared and snarled. Darius watched sadly as a large stone was pushed over the entrance — there was no escape!

Early next morning, after a sleepless night, a very worried king went straight to the lions' cave: was Daniel alive or dead? "Daniel, Daniel," he called, "Servant of the living God, has your God been able to save you?" A voice cried out from the pit. "Long live the King; my God sent his angel to shut the lions' mouths. I am not hurt at all. My God knew that I was innocent."

The king was overjoyed and ordered Daniel to be lifted out of the pit. As Darius realised that Daniel's god was the true and living God, he issued another order — to be obeyed by his people: That all should respect and worship Daniel's God, the God whose Kingdom will never be destroyed and who saves and rescues His people.

As for the chief ministers, well they suffered the fate they had wanted for Daniel.

Prayer: Father of us all, we are all important to you. Thank you for loving each and every one of us as your own special child. Help us to remember that you are the Father of all mankind, and to spread your love like rays of sunshine amongst all whom we meet every day.

Father, your name is very special. May we always speak of you with love and truth in our hearts, and show that we know and love you by the things we do. Amen.

Follow-up:
- *Make a list of all the words that could be used to describe God. Children may find some of them thinking of their own parents.*
- *Investigate ways of saying 'Father' in other languages.*

THE LORD'S PRAYER : WE ARE SORRY, LORD

Aim: *To help the children understand forgiveness: And forgive us our trespasses, as we forgive those who trespass against us. And lead us not into temptation, but deliver us from evil.*

Presentation: Have you ever done anything you know is wrong? Even a little bit! (Presenter gives an example and encourages the children to give a few.)

God is our Father and wants us to ask for things, so we can ask God to forgive us when we do things that are wrong. We know that He will forgive us if we are really sorry and are ready to forgive others. Sometimes when we are tempted to do things which we know are wrong, we think that no one knows, but God always does.

The Better Way

Linda was thirteen, she lived in a large town with her family. Dad worked in a local factory, making glass; Mum worked in an office; and Dave, her big brother, had just started working in a garage. Linda liked pop music and make-up and going out with her friends. As it was getting near Christmas time, some of her friends thought it might be fun to see how many of their presents they could 'pinch', without paying for them. "It's easy," said Debbie, "The shops are so busy no-one will notice."

This went on for a few weeks, and Linda had collected a ring, sweets, and several books. Then one day, Debbie got caught. Her parents were angry and there was a lot of fuss. Linda thought stealing was fun, but she knew that her parents would be angry too. So she stopped stealing for a while, but one day she saw a bracelet that she really wanted, so she stole it.

Just before Christmas Linda was invited to a Christian youth weekend. She met new friends, went carol singing, and learnt a lot of new things about Christmas, about giving and sharing. Linda thought a lot about what she had heard, and began to feel ashamed and unhappy about her stealing. What could she do about it? She asked one of her new friends, Lesley, "Well," said Lesley, "you must first say that you're sorry to God, our Father — then perhaps you could take the things back to the shops." Take them back! Must she really do that? thought Linda — how could she explain it all? Linda felt very worried. The more she thought about it the more she realised that she had been wrong. Linda resolved that she would give up stealing, and she would start by owning up and taking back all the presents she had stolen.

Next day, feeling very frightened she picked up her courage and took the bus to the largest department store in the town. First she went up to the supervisor and showed her the bracelet she had stolen and explained why she had brought it back. "Come with me," said the supervisor."We will have to see the manager about this." At the manager's office Linda was told to wait outside, under the watchful eye of a secretary. After five minutes, which seemed like five hours to Linda, the security manager arrived and Linda was called into the office.

"Now then," said Mr. Peel, "You had better tell us your story, I must say this is the first time that anyone has actually owned up and returned the items." Slowly Linda told the two men and the supervisor her story, how she thought that stealing had been 'fun' until someone was caught and how her weekend with new friends had changed her ideas, and now how sorry she was for having stolen her presents. At the end Mr. Peel said "Thank you, Linda. You have been very honest with us; you must realise that we usually call the police in shoplifting cases, but as the bracelet is still saleable, and you have thought very hard about your behaviour, in this case we are willing to let you go with a very stern warning. We think you have learned your lesson."

At home Linda started making her Christmas presents and felt much happier, for now she was giving rather than taking or stealing. At Christmas time, Linda was able to give her family presents made with love and care, just as God gives us the gift of his Son. Indeed, Linda found that she had so much enjoyed making all her presents that she decided to join the craft club at school and learn how to make more interesting things for other people. Making was much more fun than stealing!

Prayer: Dear Lord, we know that you love and accept us always. We ask you to forgive us when we are unkind, unhelpful or unfair .... It is not always easy to do the right thing Lord, but when we are tempted to do what we know is wrong please help us to stop and think how WE would feel. Help us to care and make the right choice, knowing that you are with us, helping us to be one of your children.

Follow-up:
● *Discuss how we feel when we have done something to hurt someone we love — breaking Dad's fishing rod; eating a whole pie from the fridge; bullying a friend — guilty, sad, unhappy, resentful, sorry. Contrast this with the joy of forgiveness. How does the forgiver and the forgiven feel? — joyful, happy, accepted, loved, relieved.*
● *Make a Sorry/Forgiven word picture.*

THE LORD'S PRAYER : IT'S YOUR WORLD, LORD

Aim: *To help the children understand about the kingdom of God and how we can help towards its coming.*

Aids: *Some third world pictures of children who are hungry, e.g. Christian Aid posters.*

Presentation: What is a KINGDOM? land, possessions, riches etc. Who rules over a kingdom? king. What makes a good king? fair, just, kind, etc.

What would God's kingdom be like? (Ask for children's ideas). Here is one person's vision:

> Wolves and sheep will live together in peace,
>   and leopards will lie down with young goats.
> Calves and lion cubs will feed together, and
>   little children will take care of them.
> Cows and bears will eat together, and their
>   calves and cubs will lie down in peace.
> Lions will eat straw as cattle do.
> Even a baby will not be harmed if it plays
>   near a poisonous snake.
> On Zion, God's sacred hill, there will be
>   nothing harmful or evil.
> The land will be as full of knowledge of
>   the LORD
>   as the seas are full of water.
>
> Isaiah 11 : v 6–9 GNB

We can all do our part to make God's kingdom here on earth.

We ask God to give us our daily bread, in His kingdom none would be hungry as many children are today. We all have a part to play in our work to make sure food reaches everyone.

A Job — or an Adventure

There was once a man who was bored with his job. He worked in a factory, where his task was to make little metal parts to go into tractors for India. All day long he had to stand at a machine, making the same little part over and over and over again, hundreds and hundreds of them; and every day he grew more bored with the work. He would watch the clock all day, longing for the time when his work would be finished and he could go home.

But one day he began to think. He thought of all the hungry people in the world, and how the tractors into which his little parts were to go could help them to grow more food, so that they would not be so hungry. A little rhyme ran in his brain:

> Without this part, the tractor won't go;
> Without the tractor, the food won't grow.

and he began to feel quite different about his work. By it he could help to bring an answer to the hunger in the world. So it became, no longer a boring job, but a real adventure; and he began really to enjoy turning out the little parts as quickly and as well as possible.

Prayer:

Children	It's not fair!
Leader	.... that some should over-eat while others die of hunger.
Children	It's not fair!
Leader	.... that people should suffer for the colour of their skin.
Children	It's not fair!
Leader	.... that men in war should kill their brothers.
Children	It's not fair!
Leader	.... that people should be lonely in the family of God.
Children	It's not fair!
Leader	.... that we should do nothing except say It's not fair!

Dear Heavenly Father, your plan is for a world of happy people, serving one another in love. We want to work with you, to bring about your kingdom on earth. Show us what we can do to help. Amen.

Follow-up:
- *Discuss the relationship between war and famine.*
- *Illustrate the reading from Isaiah.*

THE LORD'S PRAYER : WE PRAISE YOU, LORD

Aim: *To help the children understand the spirit of praise.*

Aids: *Groups of children with appropriate letter cards could form the words THANKS, PRAISE, HONOUR.*

Presentation: Today we come to give praise and joyful thanks and honour to God for His very being with us, always listening and loving us. For we know that he is always with us, providing, helping and answering our prayers. We are living in God's world, and today come to give back our love and joy for all that we have received.

A Japanese modern translation of the 23rd Psalm:

> The Lord is my pace setter.
> I shall not rush.
> He makes me stop and rest for quiet intervals,
> He provides me with images of stillness
> which restore my serenity.
> He leads me in ways of efficiency,
> Through calmness of mind,
> And his guidance is peace.
> Even though I have a great many things
> To accomplish each day
> I will not fret,
> For his presence is here,
> His timelessness, his all importance
> Will keep me in balance.
> He prepares refreshment and renewal
> In the midst of my activity
> By anointing my mind
> With his oils of tranquillity
> My cup of joyous energy overflows.
> Surely harmony and effectiveness
> Shall be the fruits of my hours,
> For I shall walk in the pace of my Lord
> and dwell in his house for ever.

We need to be quiet to experience God's presence (a short silence). And we also need to thank and praise him for all his gifts.

Prayer: Let us say Thank you to our Lord God today for all his good gifts to us each and every day.

> For shiny brown chestnuts, beautiful pictures
> in books, and patterns in marbles
> > Thank you Lord God.
> For music to dance to, Mum's voice calling us
> to tea, and for the birds singing in the morning
> > Thank you Lord God.
> For the taste of good food, clear clean water,
> and our own favourite sweets
> > Thank you Lord God.
> For sausages frying over the fire, the purr of
> the cat, and the rustle of autumn leaves under our feet
> > Thank you Lord God.
> For soft, clean clothes, the warmth of the sun on our
> faces, and the love of our family and friends
> > Thank you Lord God our Father.

Follow-up:
- *Group work. Each group could find a different way of offering praise: song, dance, mime, art, writing, to be presented in front of others, e.g. "We praise you in the morning," a collage of the seven days of creation.*
- *Make thank-you cards for parents, grandparents or others who are important to the children.*

HARVEST IN THE OLD TESTAMENT

Aim: *To explore Old Testament methods of harvest. To learn to share what is God's gift to us.*

Background: *It was the Jewish custom that the closest male member of a family should marry the widow of a close relative. Hence Boaz, being a relative of Naomi's family, was responsible for marrying and caring for Ruth.*

Aids: *Have ready large sketches, or children to mime the following activities, reaping, threshing, sifting, grinding, and let the others guess what they are doing. You will also need a piece of unleavened bread.*

Presentation: The presenter holds up a piece of unleavened bread, explaining that harvest in other countries and in other times can be very different from our own celebrations. In Old Testament Palestine there was often famine, when the crops didn't grow, and people found it very hard to collect the grain to be ground into flour.

The Story of Ruth

There was famine in the country of Moab; the harvest had failed and there was very little to eat. Naomi was unhappy; she was a widow, and now her two sons had died as well. She would go back to her real home she decided, as she had heard from friends in Bethlehem that they had had a plentiful harvest, with more than enough food for everyone.

Naomi told her plans to Orpah and Ruth, her daughters-in-law, girls from Moab who had married her sons. They both loved Naomi very much and cried "We will go with you." So they all started out on the journey together. On the way, Naomi said to the girls "You must go back to your own country to find new husbands and make new lives for yourselves." Both the girls were extremely unhappy at this and wept bitterly for they did not want to leave Naomi. Finally, Orpah kissed Naomi goodbye and returned to her mother. But Ruth was most determined and refused to do this: "Where you go, I shall go; your people shall be my people, and your God, my God," she said.

Naomi and Ruth journeyed on together and eventually reached Bethlehem where they caused great excitement. Could this really be Naomi, after all this time? How different she looked, and who was this stranger with her? Friends gave them a room and Ruth and Naomi settled down into their new life. Now it was harvest time in Bethlehem, and many of the women went gleaning in the cornfields, that is picking up the stray ears of corn so that they could grind them into flour for baking. Ruth also went out to glean and it so happened that she went into a field belonging to a farmer named Boaz.

Later in the morning, Boaz himself came into the field. Seeing Ruth he asked one of his labourers who she was. "This girl is Naomi's daughter-in-law," he said. "She has left her own country and come to look after Naomi in Bethlehem. She has worked hard all the day to take corn home so that they might have food to eat." Boaz thought well of this and he told Ruth that she might work in his fields for as long as the harvest lasted, and that she must eat with his women and be looked after by them. Ruth bowed low before him "I thank you good master," she said. "But why are you so kind to me, a foreigner?" "I have heard how good you have been to Naomi," he replied. "Now you must take plenty of corn back to her. I will tell my men to leave enough for you to pick up." So at the end of the day Ruth took a large bundle of corn home to Naomi and when she told her whose field she had been working in Naomi became very excited. "Well, dear Boaz! He is a good man, a close relative you know, and responsible for caring for us. Yes, the Lord always keeps His promises. Now we shall be well looked after."

As the harvest continued, Naomi told Ruth that it was time that she had another husband. "Remember Boaz," she said. "It is his duty to care for you," and she sent Ruth to Boaz when he was in the threshing barn to tell him of this. Ruth did as Naomi told her and Boaz was very pleased that she, a foreigner, had looked to him, when she could have looked for a husband among other men. "I am willing to marry you," he told Ruth. So Boaz married Ruth. They were very happy together and later had a son, a grandson for Naomi. Ruth's love for Naomi had made her willing to go into a strange country and trust that Naomi's God would take care of her.

Prayer: Lord God, and Father of us all, we give you grateful thanks for all of our harvest; the harvest of the field and garden, of the sea, and of the mines, and for all your good gifts to us.

We remember Ruth, and harvesters everywhere, and all their hard work which is necessary to reap food for us all to share.

We thank you too, for the harvest of men, that we may be of service to each other, and share among all people, the good news of your love.   Amen.

Follow-up:
- *Make Corn Dollies and investigate their symbolism.*
- *Visit a farm and have the farmer explain how he harvests, what each piece of machinery does.*

THANKSGIVING FOR AUTUMN

Aim: *To help the children appreciate the change of seasons and the beauty in each.*

Aids: *This assembly is intentionally simple so that slides or posters illustrating the poem may be used. Also, a percussion band might improvise a sound symphony for each verse.*

Presentation: There are many things for which we can give thanks to God in the season of autumn: brightly coloured leaves, crunching and crackling under our feet; shiny brown conkers; smoky smells of garden bonfires; the quietness of deserted holiday beaches and animals scurrying to hoard their winter stores (ask the children for further examples).

Year

Spring
Flowers blossom and bloom:
Yellow.
Trees
Preparing for summer:
A light green
Nature and man
Ready to face a new year

Summer
Flowers fully grown:
Every colour.
Richer than spring
Trees
Also
A rich dark green
Blue skies
and men in white
playing cricket,

colourful spectators
Like 'liquorice allsorts'
Watching the game.

Autumn
Flowers now scarce
Trees: semi-bare.
Brown leaves
Withered and crisp
waiting to fall
The world all set for

Winter
No flowers
No colour
Trees totally naked
Like skeletons:
Once alive
Now dead
The world seeming
so joyless ....

Until

Suddenly

Spring
Flowers blossom and bloom
Yellow
Trees
Preparing for summer
A light green

John Perry aged 12 years from *Fresh Voices,* compiled by
Donald Hilton

Prayer: Autumn is a very important part of God's natural cycle for the world, for without it spring could not reappear, and we give thanks for this by saying:

Loving Father of us all, thank you for all the beauty that the season of autumn brings. Thank you for (include some of the children's ideas mentioned earlier).

Help us to remember that all the wonders of nature are a part of your creation, and are a gift, given for us to enjoy and to preserve for those who come after us. Amen.

Follow-up:
• *Have an autumn scavenger hunt, searching for acorns, yellow leaves, conkers, beachnuts, hips, haws and hedgehogs.*
• *Make leaf prints on cloth by spraying or spattering techniques.*

MAKING PREPARATIONS FOR WINTER

Aim: *To be aware of the needs of animals during this season, and to be thoughtful in caring for them.*

Aids: *Posters of hibernating animals, some nuts.*

Presentation: Autumn is a time for making preparations. How do we prepare for the coming winter? (warm clothes, food, garden preparation. Ask the children for ideas.)

Animals and birds also need to make preparations for the coming of winter, some migrate to warmer climates. Dormice and hedgehogs hibernate through the long, cold winter months, while we might see others on warmer winter days, renewing their stores.

Some of our pets too need special care in the autumn and winter; tortoises need a warm box of hay in which to hibernate for the winter.

Poem

Thank you Lord, for the chattering squirrel,
as he leaps from tree to tree,
the scuttling dormouse, looking for his grains of corn;
the swallow as he sings high in the sky,
saying goodbye until — next year;
and my pet tortoise, as he curls up inside his shell.

Story

The Animals Prepare for Autumn

One bright, crisp autumn morning in a garden full of chestnut trees and chrysanthemums, an old stately tortoise was taking a last walk before his long winter sleep. It had been a pleasant summer, and now all around him there were fading flowers and falling conkers. He was looking forward to his box of hay and a nice warm sleep.

As Sir Toby Tortoise Esq. rustled among the crackly leaves he heard another rustle, and up poked what at first glance looked like a leafy ball, which shook itself violently to reveal a little black pointed head, with bright black eyes and a sharp nose. "Hey! You're walking over my bed!" said the squeaky voice. It was a hedgehog, attempting to make his winter nest. "I do beg your pardon, young hedgehog, sir. Getting ready for our long sleep are we? Well, I'll give you a hand then."

So together they worked, Sir Toby pushing golden brown leaves into piles with his snout, and hedgehog flattening them down with his sturdy little feet. Eventually, they had built a comfortable nest in between the long gnarled tree roots.

A loud commotion of flapping and twittering overhead drew their attention. "Are we being attacked?" said the young hedgehog in alarm. "Good gracious no," said Sir Toby, "It's only the house martins organising their last-minute flying instructions." "Why are there so many of them?" said hedgehog in amazement, as he looked out from under his covering of leaves at row upon row of black and white birds perched upon the overhead telegraph wires and chimney pots.

"They, being somewhat weaker than we four-footed beings, go abroad to warmer climes for the winter months. But we'll soon hear their raucous twitter come next May or June when the summer sun shines again over the gardens."

Suddenly, an acorn dropped on his head, "Take cover!" said the hedgehog, as he scrabbled amongst the leaves again. Then it seemed as if it were raining acorns. Looking up, the two friends saw Rusty, the cheeky squirrel, sitting high up on a branch of an old oak tree, hurling the acorns down on the ground.

"Stop that, you young rascal!" said Sir Toby in a stern voice.

Rusty swang gracefully down the tree, leaping from branch to branch and running head first down the trunk. This made hedgehog feel quite ill as he peeped out from under his leafy cover. "Hello there," chattered the squirrel, and immediately started cracking his teeth upon an acorn. "Sorry, can't offer

you any; must keep up my stocks for the winter you know."
And he leapt around the grass picking up acorns and stuffing
them into his cheeks. Quick as a flash, Rusty darted up the
old tree trunk until he was nearly at the top. "Going to hide
his secret store, I suppose," said Sir Toby. "Greedy little
thing! We'll see him about for a bit longer yet, at least while
the sun shines. Well, my old bones are getting a bit chilly; I
must be going. See you in the spring, hedgehog, and watch out
for that cheeky squirrel!"

Slowly, Sir Toby turned himself round and plodded steadily
back towards the house, and the box of hay inviting him to his
winter bed.

"Thank you for helping me to make my winter nest," called
the hedgehog after him, as he turned around and curled himself into a ball, deep amongst the leaves and roots of the old oak
tree.

The squirrel sat high on a branch, chattering to himself: he
wasn't going to bed just yet. He had more food to collect.
Then he would find a cosy hole in the old oak tree and go to
sleep. But, if the sun should shine on a bright winter's day, he
would be out and about visiting his other friends and generally
seeing that all was well in the garden.

Prayer: Today we are thinking of the birds and animals, your
creatures, Lord, who give us all so much pleasure during the
year.

We know that you will always keep them safe in your love.
Help us to be kind to any animals or birds we may find, so that
they may be warm and fed during the long winter months
ahead, waiting for the springtime when they will wake again
and delight us with their songs. Amen.

Follow-up:
● *Prepare a net bag of fat mixed with nuts and seeds. Your
local pet shop will advise.*
● *Discuss do's and don'ts of feeding birds throughout the
winter. Here are some to start off with:*
   1 Do put food out regularly. Birds become accustomed to

finding it in the same spot, same time, each day.

2 *Bacon rind is an excellent source of fat, but do cut it up in small pieces. Birds can choke.*

3 *Make sure there is a bowl of water in freezing weather. Birds need water to drink as well as food.*

4 *Brown bread is better for birds — and people. White bread is filling, but not nourishing.*

ARE THINGS REALLY DYING?

Aids: *Bulbs, fibre and pots for planting. A large OHP or sketch of the cut section of a bulb.*

Presentation: *Presenter shows the bulbs to the children:* These look dead, but what is inside? (Food). Explains diagram, that the bulb is a food store for the roots and next year's leaves. Here is something which looks dead, but is really alive and waiting to be given the right conditions to grow and blossom. How can we make these dead-looking bulbs come really alive? (Conditions needed for growth: light, air, warmth, darkness, water and care.) *In a small group, the children might help to plant the bulbs.*

What other things seem to be dying in the autumn. (Trees shedding leaves, flowers.) They are really storing and using their food to prepare for the winter and the hope of growth and blossom the following spring.

In a Christian group, the presenter might make the following point: We need to be like the bulbs, dying too, and giving up the things which we know are wrong about our lives, asking God for his help if we want to follow Christ and have new, fresh lives, which will blossom like the spring flowers.

Nicodemus

Have you ever been afraid that your friends might laugh at you? Perhaps you've been given a new pair of 'sensible' shoes which are not really in fashion, and you know that you have to wear them or Granny will be upset. Well, Nicodemus felt a bit like that. For many weeks he had been on the edge of the crowd, listening to Jesus talk. He was very interested in what Jesus was saying; he felt that he would like to learn more, but how could he do it? If he visited Jesus openly by day his friends would most certainly question and laugh at him. Nicodemus was one of the Jewish leaders in Jerusalem and would not be expected to mix with peasants from Galilee. So he would have to visit Jesus at night, and he would need to plan this very carefully so that no one would know.

Late at night, Nicodemus dressed himself in a long black cloak, and crept stealthily along the dark streets to the house where Jesus was staying: should he knock, or should he go home? As he knocked softly, he saw the flickering light of a candle and Jesus himself opened the door. "Ah, Nicodemus, I was expecting you," said Jesus.

As they sat at the table together Nicodemus felt more relaxed: "Rabbi," he said, "Some of us know that you are the teacher sent by God; how can we find out more about God for ourselves?"

"Well," said Jesus, "you must look around you, at the people you meet and the things that happen every day to see God working in his world. You can find God in your relationships with other people, rather than in keeping all the rules. You hear and see God at work yet you refuse to believe his message. I am telling you the truth," said Jesus. "No-one can see the Kingdom of God unless he is born again." This answer puzzled Nicodemus very much, for how could this be possible; he couldn't be born again, could he?

"Of course," said Jesus, "I mean a rebirth and change of your feelings towards other people, and in the way you live your life. Let God's love and power help you to live the life that he wants you to live. Then you will be able to see how God really works. If you accept God then you must believe in the Son also."

So, as Nicodemus went away with much to think about, he felt himself on the brink of a great change. For the next few months he continued to follow Jesus at a distance until the events of Easter forced him to make a decision, about Jesus and the way that he would live his life. But that's another story ....

Prayer:
For misty morn
and quiet eve
For swallow ranks
About to leave,
We thank you, heavenly Father.

For life mature,
For red and brown,
For next year's plants
As seeds come down,
We thank you, heavenly Father.

This is the rhythm of life, Lord.
To you be all glory and praise.

From *Prayers to use with 8–11's*

Follow-up

● *Make a date chart for the bulbs planted.*

● *Make a collage of pond life as a further instance that things are not what they seem. Ponds often seem empty until you know where to look for things.*

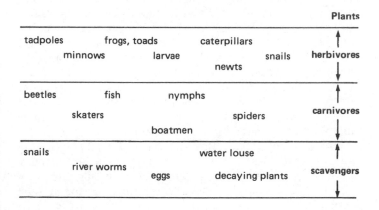

				Plants
tadpoles	frogs, toads	caterpillars		↑
minnows	larvae	snails		**herbivores**
	newts			↓
beetles	fish	nymphs		↑
skaters	spiders			**carnivores**
boatmen				↓
snails	water louse			↑
river worms				**scavengers**
eggs	decaying plants			↓

BONFIRE NIGHT

Preventive Medicine

Aim: *One current issue at this time of the year is the safety of fireworks and bonfires. The following story and prayer aims to help children to enjoy the beauty and fellowship of such an occasion, but at the same time to be aware of the safety aspects involved, and to care for those who are accidentally injured at such times.*

Aids: *A Guy, a box of matches.*

Presentation:

Bonfire Night

Miss Holmes was telling the children about Guy Fawkes, Robin was feeling sad, for Mum would not let him take a Guy around the streets to collect for pennies. Mum did not approve of begging. So Robin was very cross as he kicked the falling leaves around on his way home. In the garden, his ten-year-old sister Sally was looking at a heap of leaves which a hedgehog was busy making into his winter quarters. Robin said he wanted to have a bonfire like his schoolfriends; Sally said they would not be able to, because Dad was away working on an oil rig. Also the pile of leaves was too near the fence; and anyway, the hedgehog had made it his home now!

Mum did not like fireworks; in fact she was frightened of them. Their garden was too small for fireworks, she said. Next door, Mr Coombes was tidying up his jumbly garden, and there in the middle was a big pile of rubbish. "Going to have a bonfire?" asked Robin. "May be," said Mr Coombes. "On Guy Fawkes night?" Robin went on. "We'll see," said Mr Coombes. "I may be on duty; some people do very silly things on Bonfire Night." Mr Coombes was a member of the St John Ambulance Brigade, and the children had often seen him go off on duty in his smart uniform.

Next Saturday Mr Coombes called over the fence to the children, "I have an idea; we'll collect more rubbish for the fire and then we can have a big bonfire for Guy Fawkes night, and have a collection for the St John Ambulance."

At school, Robin enlisted fourteen friends to help him collect rubbish from around the neighbourhood for the huge bonfire. Dad's weekly letter arrived with a cheque for the children to buy some fireworks, so Mum went with them to the local shop where they decided what to have: rockets, falling rain, crackers and catherine wheels. Mrs Coombes was busy making a poster which said "Grand street Guy Fawkes Bonfire – Adults 10p, Children 5p." Mum suggested that they made a Guy, so Sally found an old potato sack, a pair of Dad's old trousers, a balloon for his head, and an old dunce's hat. She stuffed the sack and trousers with newspapers.

When bonfire night arrived, Sally tied an old piece of clothes line from the hedge to the apple tree to keep the crowd from the hedgehog's leaves. "All the children on Sally's side of the fence. We don't want any accidents," said Mr Coombes as he put a taper to the fire. Whoosh! Great sparks shot up. The Guy caught fire. Bang! That was his head gone! Soon the bonfire was a roaring crackling leafy mass of flames. Mr Coombes used one of Dad's old garden rakes to keep the burning paper from blowing around, then he began to set off the fireworks. It was a really super show. When the bonfire died down, Mrs Coombes made cocoa for everyone and Mr Coombes said that they had made £5 for the St John Ambulance Brigade, to help any unfortunate people who did have accidents. When they got home Robin said the *he* was going to become a St John Ambulance cadet when he was nine.

Prayer: Loving Lord God, we praise you for all the beautiful colours and excitement of the bonfire and fireworks – for the zooming rockets, as they speed high up into the sky, for the crackle and fizz of the bangers, and the sparkling patterns of the catherine wheels. We remember too, that fire and fireworks can be dangerous as well as fun, and we give you thanks for all who teach us to use the Firework Code, and who help us to enjoy Bonfire night safely (men and women of the St John Ambulance Brigade, the Red Cross, club leaders, parents).

May we remember any who suffer accidents at this time, and pray that you will be with them in their recovery. Help us always to be careful at bonfire parties, so that Guy Fawkes night may be a safe and happy evening for everyone. Amen.

Follow-up:
● *Tell a simple version of the story of Guy Fawkes.*
● *Make a class Guy, and collect for a charity.*
● *Publicise community bonfires, which are much safer than individual ones.*

MEDICINE

St Luke, October 19th

Background: *Luke, or Lucanus was a Greek, a Roman citizen, son of a former slave to an important Roman soldier, Diodorus Cyrinius, who became his adopted father.*

Lucanus trained as a physician, a doctor, but instead of treating the rich, he felt that it was his duty to heal those who could not afford the help of a physician, especially those slaves in the many galley ships which surrounded the ports of the Mediterranean: also prisoners and the very poor in these cities.

Luke had been taught about God, or the Unknown god of the Greeks, as he had known him, as a child by Keptah, his former Roman family's slave physician. As he grew up he found himself arguing with God: why did God allow disease and misery and death amongst mankind? He was Luke's enemy, not his Father.

Later in his life, Luke discovered that it was God who was working miracles through the gift of healing given to Luke — (see story) and also about this time Luke began hearing tales of Jesus of Nazareth, and remembered much that Keptah had told him of the birth of the Messiah.

After the crucifixion, Luke began to search for the followers of Jesus, and wrote down many of the stories which were later to become St Luke's Gospel.

Presentation: In the time shortly after Jesus had lived on earth, Lucanus was a physician to a large Roman ship captained by a man named Gallo. He was a doctor to the passengers, for the slaves would have no one to care for them on such a ship. During the voyage, Lucanus realised that there was plague on board, a most painful and deadly disease. After a while the captain agreed that this was so, but the disease was only among the galley slaves, slaves, not men; they didn't matter. But to Lucanus they mattered very much: all were God's children.

One night, having covered himself in linen cloths, to protect himself from the disease, Lucanus and his servant Cusa went deep down into the part of the ship where it was very dark, cold and evil smelling; where they found row upon row of slaves, men, women and children, lying chained together, all suffering, and many dying of the plague. Lucanus took packets of medicine and pails of water and gave each sick slave a sip of the medicine. He spoke gently and lovingly to each person, and did what he could to ease the pain of the dying. He gave the overseer more disinfectant and medicine with orders that the slaves and the rooms be washed down at intervals, and all the rats be killed. Forgetting that he too might catch the deadly disease, Lucanus returned for several days to tend his patients. Slowly some of the slaves responded, they knew that Lucanus loved them and wanted to help them. Three days later he was summoned to the captain's cabin; the illness had gone, "It was not plague after all," said the captain, but Lucanus knew that it had been, and realised that God had used him to bring about a miracle.

Prayer: Dear Father, as we remember the story of St Luke, his love and gift of healing, we pray for all who are involved in healing, nurses, physiotherapists, radiographers, speech therepists and dieticians. We think especially of the doctors who have learned to heal the sick and to take away pain.

We ask for your blessing upon all who are involved in medical research, and for medical missionaries who are working to help overcome disease and ill health in different parts of the world. Lord, help them to show your love to the sick, so that they may know that you are near and caring for them. Amen.

Follow-up:
● *Project on Hospital workers. The following details may be used as the basis for a large mural or collage. Explain them to the children first.*

Physiotherapist: *helps patients become mobile after having broken bones, arthritis, rheumatism. Gives exercises for specific complaints: swimming, working in the gymnasium, heat treatment. Helps children with crutches to walk again.*

Radiographer: *diagnostic and therapeutic radiographers. Diognostic — work with patients requiring x-rays for diagnosis — usually works in a radiography unit within a hospital. Therapeutic — works with patients requiring radiation treatment.*

Ward Receptionist: *greets incoming patients, takes initial details, takes medical notes and takes them to department where needed. Helps with some auxiliary nursing duties.*

Dietician: *plans special diets for various illnesses, e.g. diabetics. Lectures student nurses in dietry needs. Explains special diets to patients concerned, and helps them to plan for themselves.*

Porter: *various transport jobs, taking people to theatre, beds and wheelchairs to where they are needed; moves food from kitchens to wards and transports laundry.*

Electrician: *concerned with all the electrical safety in the hospital, maintaining all electrical equipment in wards, labs, theatres.*

Domestics: *responsible for the cleanliness of all wards, hoovering, polishing.and dusting; often talk to patients.*

WRVS: *runs voluntary shops, brings trolleys to wards, brings library books, sometimes visits lonely patients.*

● *Ask one or more of the above to come and demonstrate their skills. Nurses and physiotherapists are the most accessible.*

A STAY IN HOSPITAL

Aim: *Some children are very afraid of going into hospital, and of not knowing what is going to happen to them there. This story tries to assuage these fears and to show children that a stay in hospital can be quite fun after all; a place where one is lovingly cared for, where parents can often stay the night as well as the day, and where one can make many new friends.*

Aids: *A pair of crutches; any pupil who happens to have on a plaster cast.*

Presentation: It was the first day of the long summer holidays, Barry was looking forward to going camping with the Youth Club. As it was a bright, sunny morning Barry decided to climb up into his tree 'hide'. This was his special place, which he had made himself during the long summer evenings, constructed out of old planks of wood, branches, an old counterpane, and the wheel from the broken garden wheelbarrow. It had changed its shape on many occasions, to become a ship, a castle, or a spaceship.

Today, he decided, it would be a look-out post in the jungle, and as he sat planning an expedition he suddenly heard a strange noise coming from higher up in the branches. It was a cross between a scream and a whistle — there is went again. Barry decided to investigate. Looking out of his special 'window' (a hole cut out of the moth-eaten counterpane!), to his amazement, Barry saw a brilliantly coloured parrot! He blinked and looked again; yes, it really was a parrot. Barry decided that he must catch this parrot. So, taking a few biscuits from his secret store, he began to crawl very quietly and carefully out of his hide, along the branch. The parrot, meanwhile, sat watching him. Hand over hand Barry crawled, just like they'd been taught at school. He was just in touching distance of the bird, when the parrot flapped its wings and flew away, out of the tree, through a cascade of falling leaves. The vibration of the branch made Barry lose his grip, and he too, slipped and fell out of the tree, crashing through the branches as he went, until he hit the ground with a terrific bump! Ooh ... did it hurt.

Barry's father, hearing all the noise, and having seen the parrot fly out of the tree, rushed to where Barry was lying in a heap on the ground. When he found Barry was unable to walk he called an ambulance and very soon Barry found himself being whisked off to hospital with two very worried parents.

Once at the hospital the doctors and nurses were very kind to him, gently feeling his leg all over, and taking X-rays. He had broken it very badly and would have to have it set. Then he would have to stay in hospital for a while. Barry was feeling very sad and miserable; what about his camping holiday now? Barry was taken on a trolley to the theatre, with his parents walking beside him. After a little prick, he was quickly asleep and when he awoke again it was to find himself in the children's ward, with his leg in a plaster supported in a sort of sling.

Barry's mum stayed in the hospital with him for a few days until he got used to the routine and had made some new friends. In the next bed to him was a boy called Steve who had had his appendix out. The two boys soon became friends. They found that the ward had a computer and the boys spent many happy hours playing with it. There was also a video, so they were able to watch some films. Barry's leg gradually became less painful, and soon he was able to stretch around the bed sufficiently to play games on the snooker table with some of the nurses. Barry's parents came to visit him every day, and many of his schoolfriends came too. One day, Barry had a very special visitor — the owner of the parrot, with the parrot Joey — (this time securely in a cage). All of the children thought Joey was super, and chatted away to him, trying to teach him new tricks.

The time passed quickly, for the children had a visit from some circus clowns and they even managed to have a midnight feast, with a pillow fight, which sister wasn't too pleased about the next day! Soon Barry was able to have some physiotherapy exercises to help strengthen his bone. Eventually, after one of the doctor's examinations he was given a pair of crutches and taught by the physiotherapist to walk with them. He was a bit shaky at first, but he soon got the hang of moving them. Then, the great day arrived; he could go home! Barry was overjoyed, home at long last. Mum and Dad came to collect him, and Barry said goodbye to all of his new friends and the nurses and doctors who had looked after him so well. He promised that he would be careful, and would come back again soon — just for a visit. Being in hospital wasn't so bad after all, and as for camping? Well, there was always next year.

Prayer: 1. Dear Lord, when Barry was in hospital the nurses were very kind to him. They used to play games. Lord Jesus, we remember that you made people who were ill well again, We know that nursing is important work and we thank you for all the people who help make others well. Amen.

      2. Hospitals are very busy places Lord, we remember all the many different people who work hard to make them run efficiently — porters, carpenters, cooks and cleaners, many office workers and laboratory technicians, as well as all the medical staff we see in the wards.

Help them Lord, to work well together, and to value each other's work in the business of their everyday life; and help us to say 'thank you' too when we visit our hospitals. Amen.

Follow-up:
● *Hospital drama for children. Going to hospital to have their tonsils out. Stages: child with parent(s) goes to children's ward, greeted by ward receptionist — shown bed — nurse takes details, weighs child — sister talks to parents — child goes to playroom and meets other children and playleader — examined by houseman — talks to cleaner on duty — given injection by nurse — porter arrives and child and nurse go to theatre — anaesthetist talks to child, gives another injection — surgeon performs operation assisted by various doctors and nurses — child taken back to ward by porter and nurse — wakes up in bed — parent(s) present to comfort. Later allowed drink goes back to sleep. Next day breakfast — gets up and washes, goes to playroom — temperature taken by nurse — examined by*

doctor — playroom — lessons with hospital teacher — plays with other children — nurses — lunch and goes home later that day.

● *Encourage children who have had stays in hospital to share their experiences.*

● *Practise elementary First Aid. A St John Ambulance volunteer might help.*

OUR BODIES

Aim: *To help the children understand how complex their bodies are, and to treat their bodies healthily, with respect.*

Aids: *One large nail, a bucket of water, a box of matches, and seven bars of soap. A chart showing decibel levels as described in the presentation.*

Presentation: Did you know that:—

> There is enough iron in the body of a healthy adult to make a nail 75mm long.
>
> Two-thirds of your body's weight is water. So if you weigh 40 kilos, 13.3 kilos is water.
>
> All the phosphorus in your body would make 2,000 match heads!
>
> You could make seven bars of soap with all the fat in your body.

Just think. Our bodies are composed of water, fats, protein, acids, chemicals and minerals. We could see ourselves then as a lot of bits and pieces put together like a toy model. But of course we would only be like machines. rather than live human beings. All of these substances are balanced and arranged in a most complex way to make bodies.

Let me see you all smile. That takes seventeen muscles, all working together. Now, let me see you all frown — look really annoyed. Now that took forty-three muscles. So it's easier to smile than to frown.

Your heart is a very important muscle. It pumps used blood to the lungs to be filled with oxygen, and then pumps fresh blood to all the parts of your body. Your heart begins beating before you are born and keeps on the whole of your life, about forty million times each year. And we take it all for granted. Just for a moment, feel your heart beating. Because the heart is so active and central, many cultures have thought that all our feelings came from it. Certainly, when we are excited or anxious, our heart beat speeds up and we are aware of it pumping faster.

What tells the heart to pump fast or slow is messages sent from the brain along our nerves. You can think of the system of nerves as a giant telephone exchange, with enough lines to connect every person on earth. That's a lot of lines. The messages travel along our nerves much faster than the world helicopter speed record.

We can think of the brain as a giant computer, receiving information from outside the body and recording it for future reference. Would you all raise your right arms? Thank you; you may put them down now. What you have just done, you did without really thinking. To you it is an automatic response to a simple request. But in fact, many messages passed to and from the brain to enable you to do that. How many more messages must pass along the nerves to do more difficult things like kicking a football or jumping a rope?

We have five senses: seeing with our eyes, touching with our skins, smelling with our noses, tasting with our mouths, and hearing with our ears. Ears are so important, and very delicate. Most of us know how very painful earache can be. Loud sounds can damage our ears, and it is important not to be near them for very long. Farmers who use tractors for long hours now wear earmuffs to prevent the loud motor from deafening them. Other people who have to protect their ears are men who use loud machines like drills and steam hammers, or who have to stand outside aeroplanes to direct their take-off.

Sound is measured in decibels. When we talk to each other normally, we are about 60 decibels loud. When we shout (shout this phrase), as I just did, that's about 90 decibels. A live pop group puts out a sound of about 120 decibels, and a gunshot is 140 decibels. Listening to a loud pop group all evening can damage your hearing, so be careful.

All these facts about your bodies show how interesting and complex they are, and yet we so often take bodies for granted. We ought to respect our bodies and take great care of them, eat good food, exercise the muscles and avoid harmful things like too loud sounds or silly risks that might damage them.

Prayer/Meditation:

> God thought and thought,
> Till he thought: I'll make me a man!
>
> Up from the bed of the river
> God scooped the clay;
> And by the bank of the river
> He kneeled him down;
> And there the great God Almighty,
> Who lit the sun and fixed it in the sky,
> Who flung the stars to the most far corner of the night,
> Who rounded the earth in the middle of his hand;
> This Great God,
> Like a mammy bending over his baby,
> Kneeled down in the dust
> Toiling over a lump of clay
> Till he shaped it in his own image;
>
> Then into it he blew the breath of life,
> And man became a living soul.
> Amen, Amen.

James Weldon Johnson

Dear God, you have made our bodies able to do so many things, to run and jump, to eat, and hear music, to think and wonder. Help us to respect our bodies, to keep them fit and healthy as an offering to you. Amen.

Follow-up:
- *Make fingerprints of all the class to show how each person's are different.*
- *Ask the local health visitor in to talk about a healthy diet.*

WHO IS A SAINT?

Aim: *To encourage children to develop their own desire to follow God, and to present the lives of people living and dead who have done that with their whole selves as example and inspiration.*

Background notes on Canonization: *Canonization is the method by which the Roman Catholic Church decides who is a Saint. Since the seventeenth century, this process has involved the calling of witnesses, the collection of evidence, clear signs of power of Jesus Christ in the life of the person concerned, and much discussion and searching enquiries. The Postulator presents the evidence for canonization, and the Promotor of the Faith questions the evidence. At the last of these discussions the Pope is present and, if all agree, the course for canonization goes ahead. The Saint is declared Holy or a martyr; then a servant of God. He or she is next declared blessed and finally, with a special celebration, a Saint. Usually fifty years after the candidate's death has to elapse before the process for Canonization can begin, and often the collection of evidence can take several hundred years.*

Saints are created as signs of hope, a sign that the Gospel of Jesus really does change lives.

Of course there are many people who live just such lives but are not publicly acknowledged, known to God and those they have helped.

Presentation: Who can tell me the name of a Saint? (Children's response). What can you tell me about these people, what did they do? Why do you think they are saints?

After the children's answers —

Let's see if we can find some things that are common to them all: they are all dead, they all did something special or made some sacrifice for the people or the community in which they lived; they were all Christians with a strong faith in God which directed their actions; they all tried to follow Jesus and show

God's love to those around them. Do you think there are people who might become saints today? The following story is about just one such person.

A Home for Antonio and Maria

Antonio and Maria lived in Naples, Italy. They didn't have a home because they were too poor, so they slept where they could find shelter, in shop doorways, or by railway lines.

One day they were selling matches in the streets, when along came a man called Riccardo Santi, out for a walk before tea. Pastor Santi was a Methodist minister and had a large family himself, so he loved to talk to children.

"Buy a box of matches mister," said Antonio. Pastor Santi stopped and began talking to the children. He found out that their father had died, and that their mother had to work very hard as a housemaid in one of the larger houses in the city.

"We sell matches to buy us all some food," said little Maria, rubbing her tummy hopefully. But that day they had sold no matches and hadn't eaten at all.

Pastor Santi thought back to his own childhood; he too had been poor, and an orphan, and had been brought up in a children's home. There he had always found good food and loving friends, and he felt that God was calling him to do the same here, to give these children a home.

"Well," he said, "today is a special day, for it is my birthday, and I'd like you to come home and have tea with me."

"Oh, yes," said the children together. Antonio and Maria followed Pastor Santi through the narrow streets, happy at the thought of a meal at least, for they were very hungry indeed.

Eventually they reached the Methodist centre where Pastor Santi lived with his family. They were not at all surprised to see two more guests, for the centre, although only a poor building was often 'home' for the hungry and homeless of Naples. The Santi family themselves were not at all rich and there was only just enough food to go round, but Mama Santi gladly divided this up so there was enough for the two small children. To Antonio and Maria, this meal was a feast, for during the last few days they had eaten only what they had begged from people on the streets. All the children sang "Happy Birthday" to Pastor Santi as a thank you for their meal, and eventually Mama Santi said that it was time that they found the children's mother, for she would have finished her work and would be looking for them.

Pastor Santi asked the two children if they would like to spend the night at his home, and when their mother was found she readily agreed because they had nowhere to sleep that night. Antonio and Maria stayed and had a bed for the night, for the first, the second and the third, until they found that they were living with the Santi family all the time. Soon more children arrived, and Riccardo Santi found that he was indeed creating his own children's home.

Over the years many children, the waifs and strays from Naples and surrounding villages, became part of one big happy family. They all worked together to help and care for each other. The boys cleaned shoes, and the girls helped with the cooking and sewing. Often there were problems; money was always scarce — sometimes they were in danger of being thrown out onto the streets if they couldn't pay the rent. But whatever happened, God always looked after them. Men and women of Pastor Santi's church gave food and clothes. Sometimes they were even able to give a little money, usually just when it was needed.

The Santi family grew and grew, largely because erupting volcanoes and the first World War left many children homeless. Eventually, with help from American Methodists, they moved to a large house in Portici, to be named Casa Materna — Mother's Home, where, over the following years many children were to be cared for. Pastor Santi's motto for the home was "Let the children come to me": no child has ever been turned away. These children have been loved and cared for, and educated for a living. The task of providing a home still goes on today, under the leadership of two of Pastor Santi's sons, Teofilo and Emanuelle.

Prayer: We praise you Lord, for your saints throughout the ages, for their courage, determination and example in following the life of your Son, Jesus Christ.

We thank you for all the living saints of our **own** day, especially Pastor Santi and his family in Naples, and ask that through their lives they may speak to us of your love for all your children. This we ask in the name of Jesus Christ. Amen.

Follow-up:
- *Make an ABC of saints, how far can you go?*
- *Find out about the patron saints of crafts and callings, e.g. St Bartholemew, patron saint of leather workers.*
- *Write about someone who you think is a saint.*
- *If you were asked to choose four new (modern) patron saints for our country who would you choose and why?*

HALLOWEEN

October 31st

Aim: *To discover the origins of Halloween and to explore the festival within the Christian context of Hallow tide.*

To enjoy some of the fun and games of the festival itself. To teach that light and goodness overcome evil and darkness; and that through our acceptance and response to God's love towards us, to believe that we may always walk 'in the light'.

Aids: *Darkened hall, pumpkin lanterns, children dressed as witches, suitable 'spooky' music.*

Background: *Halloween is part of the Christian festival of Hallowtide, Halloween, Holy Eve before All Saints and All Souls. Halloween has Celtic origins being originally the feast of Sanhain, the last night of the old Celtic year, when all kinds of spirits were active. It was a night of danger, of the unknown. Sanhain also signified the change from Autumn to Winter, it was the night when feasts were held for the dead and animals killed for the winter. On this night fires and lights were lit, in the belief that light had power over darkness, hence pumpkin lanterns to frighten away witches and ghosts. A custom of trick or treat began, to sweep away evil and start afresh for the coming year. Halloween games such as apple bobbing and games with nuts are said to have Roman origins. Under Christian influence, the Celtic feasts diminished and the emphasis was shifted to remembering the saints and all who had died*

Presentation: The Witches' Speech from *Macbeth* (to be mimed or acted).

> Double, double toil and trouble
> Fire burn, and cauldron bubble.
> Fillet of a fenny snake,
> In the cauldron boil and bake;

Eye of newt and toe of frog,
Wool of bat, and tongue of dog,
Adder's fork and blind worm's sting,
Lizard's leg and howlet's wing —
For a charm of pow'rful trouble
Like a hell-broth boil and bubble.
Double, double toil and trouble
Fire burn and cauldron bubble.

Children bring on some lit pumpkin lanterns and witches
with a cry sink in a heap, afraid of the light. Main lights are
put on, and pumpkins put to one side.

The good light overcomes the evil of the darkness and the
witches. Tell of the background to Halloween.

Halloween

This is the night when witches fly
on their whizzing broomsticks through
the wintry sky;
Steering up the pathway where the
stars are strewn,
They stretch skinny fingers to the
waking moon.

This is the night when old wives tell
strange and creepy stories, tales of charm
and spell,
Peering at the pictures flaring in
the fire
They wait for whispers from a
ghostly choir.

This is the night when angels go
In and out the houses, winging
O'er the snow;
Clearing out the demons from
the countryside

They make it new and ready for
Christmastide.

Leonard Clark, in *Times' Delights*

Prayer: Dear Heavenly Father, we give you thanks for the protective lights of the world around us, street lamps, traffic lights, lighthouses and the miners' safety lamp.

We ask that you will protect us from all that is evil in our lives, and lead us to follow your Light, shining ever before us. Help us not to be afraid of the dark, but to rest knowing that we are always held in your caring love. Amen.

Follow-up:
- *Find out about the other days of Hallowtide, All Saints and All Souls.*
- *Have a Saints and Witches party.*
- *Some children will have fears about witches and ghosts. Discussion and explanation may be necessary to allay these.*

ST ANDREW

November 30th

Aim: *To explain how Andrew came to be connected with Scotland. To explore the idea of the missionary.*

Aids: *Either a flag or a picture of the Union Jack, or St Andrew's flag of Scotland; a map or globe.*

Presentation: Ask how many of the children are called Andrew? Explain the flag, pointing out the diagonal white cross which symbolises purity and the blue background, symbolising the sea, which St Andrew, a fisherman loved. Ask the children of which country St Andrew is the patron saint. Here is how he came to be the patron saint of Scotland.

Andrew, a disciple of Jesus, was a fisherman with Peter in Galilee. He was one of the first disciples to be called 'fishers of men'. One other thing we find from the Bible is that it was Andrew who brought the boy with the loaves and fishes to Jesus so that five thousand might be fed.

During the first century Andrew was a missionary, he travelled in Syria, Turkey, and Russia, as far as the Black Sea and the river Volga, (find on globe), making many Christian converts. Finally he was taken prisoner on Patros, one of the Greek islands. The wife of the Roman Proconsul had become a Christian, which had upset her husband very much. This new Christianity seemed to be turning the people against the old gods, so the proconsul ordered Andrew's arrest and crucifixion to free his part of the country from this new religion.

Andrew thought himself unworthy to be crucified in the same way as Christ, so his cross was a diagonal. Legend tells us that he preached and talked to people for many hours from his cross as he was dying and made many more converts. His bones were taken to Constantinople from Patros (where he died) and remained there for many years and it was during this time that he was recognised as a saint.

One night, hundreds of years later, in the sixth century, an old monk called Regulus, who was in charge of Andrew's grave at Constantinople, had a strange dream. He was visited by an angel who told him to find a safe resting place for Andrew's bones. So, with a group of monks, Regulus set sail for he knew not where. He had a long journey across many seas (use globe to point this out). He often felt lonely and thought of his home country. He encountered rough seas and storms, when the wind blew and the waves roared, rocking the small boat from side to side. Regulus prayed to God that they might reach land in safety. Eventually, they reached the east coast of Scotland.

Regulus was so pleased to reach land at last that he immediately knelt on the ground and gave thanks to God. Then the monks built an altar of stones over the casket of bones. As the monks stayed to teach the people about God and Jesus Christ, a church and then a fine cathedral were built over the spot where St Andrew's bones lay buried. You may still visit the Cathedral of St Andrew in the city named after him; and that is the story of how St Andrew became adopted as the patron saint of Scotland and the special saint of all missionaries.

Prayer: Father of all, as we think of St Andrew, we pray for all missionaries who have travelled to faraway countries to bring the good news of your love to many people. Help them to be always aware of your presence and give them the strength to deal with their problems.

We give you thanks for all the various missionary societies, (CMS, USPG and any others) who send their workers to help all over the world, and ask that through them lives may be helped, and that more people may come to know of you and your love.   Amen.

Follow-up:
● *Have a St Andrew's Day celebration. Make flags, short-bread; have Scottish music and learn a simple Scottish dance.*
● *All missionary societies are able to provide speakers. Contact any local church to be put in touch. Many clergy now in England have at one time worked abroad as missionaries.*

CELEBRATING AND REMEMBERING

Birthdays and Remembrance Day

Aim: *To question WHY we remember particularly people, and to share in celebrating a common occasion when we do remember friends and family. Remembrance Sunday continues the theme of remembering — remembering for a different reason, that of respect for a cause or deed, and is something positive, rather than just accepting what has been done in the past.*

Aids: *One or two large Birthday cards, Remembrance Day poppies.*

Presentation: Think of a day that we can each look forward to, and which we can celebrate with our friends *(hold up birthday cards)*.

Why do we remember various people's birthdays?

Family Birthdays

My brother's birthday is in April
 Spring flowers come out,
My sister's in January,
Snow round about,
Father was born at the end of June,
They were cutting the hay;
Mother on the first of August,
A very hot day;
January, April, June and August,
So we go through the year
January snow, June's dust
Soon *my* birthday will be here,
It is an easy one to remember
The twenty fifth of December.

Leonard Clark, *Collected Poems and Verse for Children*

84

What do we especially like to remember on our birthdays? (the time of year, birthday cards, presents, parties, getting older/bigger. If possible use this time to let a birthday child explain his/her particular enjoyments, or to wish a child a happy birthday).

Why else do we often remember particular people? (Because they have done a brave deed.) Next Sunday is Remembrance Sunday, when we especially remember all those soldiers, sailors and airman of all nations who fought and gave their lives in past wars, while serving their country. *(Show poppies.)* These poppies represent the lives of all these men, and that is why you will often see people wearing poppies at this time. Money collected from their sale goes towards caring for those men who are having to live in special homes, or who need special medical care because of their wounds.

Prayer: Lord Jesus Christ, thank you for the special days which we like to remember and joyfully celebrate, especially our own birthdays and those of our family and friends. May we always remember them for what they mean to us.

Help us to remember also with love and thanksgiving, those who have given much for their country, for — "They shall not grow old, as we that are left grow old. Age shall not weary them, nor the years condemn. At the going down of the sun, and in the morning, we will remember them."

Follow-up:
● *What else can we remember about our lives? Look at the poem "I Remember" by Thomas Hood.*
● *See how much you can find out about life in the past or your local community by an 'I remember' investigation. Ask parents, grandparents, clergy, shopkeepers.*
● *Discuss what sort of practical things might be done to remember, or commemorate particular people in your school or area.*

MARRIAGE OF A MEMBER OF STAFF

Aim: *To share the joy and happiness of the couple; a link with the school as family; to begin to understand the importance of marriage and commitment. Invite both the member of staff and spouse to attend the assembly.*

Presentation: Introduce the couple to the school and convey good wishes of joy and happiness. Presenter or one of the engaged couple begins a question and answer session with the children — What do they think of at a wedding? What happens at a wedding? and what is really important at a wedding? Allow time for free discussion and for the couple to tell the children what actually did happen at their wedding. Perhaps they could share photographs. Be prepared for questions about falling in love.

Reading (1):   Love

I may be able to speak the languages of men and even of angels, but if I have no love, my speech is no more than a noisy gong or a clanging bell.

I may have the gift of inspired preaching; I may have all knowledge and understand all secrets; I may have all the faith needed to move mountains — but if I have no love, I am nothing.

I may give away everything I have, and even give up my body to be burnt — but if I have no love, this does me no good.

Love is patient and kind; it is not jealous or conceited or proud; love is not ill-mannered or selfish or irritable; love does not keep a record of wrongs; love is not happy with evil, but is happy with the truth.

Love never gives up; and its faith, hope, and patience never fail.

                                    1 Corinthians 13:1—7 GNB

Reading (2): **The Vows**

Name, will you take *Name* to be your wife? Will you love her, comfort her, honour and protect her, and, forsaking all others, be faithful to her as long as you both shall live?

Name, will you take *Name* to be your husband? Will you love him, comfort him, honour and protect him, and, forsaking all others, be faithful to him as long as you both shall live?

The answer to these questions is, I will.

Prayer:
Give us love Lord,
Whatever we do
Show us kindness Lord,
Whatever we do
We need your love Lord,
Whatever we do
Show us mercy Lord
Whatever we do

Guard us daily Lord
Whatever we do
We'll keep on praying Lord
Whatever we do
Love is powerful Lord
Whatever we do
We'll love you strongly Lord
Whatever we do

From *Assembly Workshop* by Gillian Catu

Follow-up:
- *There may well be children in the group whose parents have separated or divorced. Encourage them to express their ideas about marriages having difficulties. Be sure to reassure them that it is not the children's fault.*
- *Begin a project on wedding customs in different cultures.*
- *Make up a piece of percussion or a song for a wedding.*

THE BIRTH OF A BABY

Member of staff or pupil's family

Aim: *Welcoming a new member of the 'family' — sharing a joyful occasion — gaining an insight into the responsibilities of parenthood and family life. Invite mother or both parents and new baby to come to the assembly.*

Presentation: Today we are very pleased to welcome Mr/Mrs — — and baby — — to our school. Either — — has a new baby brother/sister or Mrs — — used to teach class — — and we share with them a new member of the family.

They are going to tell us a little about the new baby:

Presenter promotes questions from the children about name, weight, age, how baby is looked after, how the parents' lives have changed, what the baby eats, what skills the baby has, what sort of personality.

The children might wish to sing a song for the baby.

Poem

Tight pink fingers and curled up toes,
A screwed up nose and a cry in the night,
Father God we have a new baby in the family!
Every time we look at him/her it makes
us feel warm and happy inside.

From *Prayers for 8–11's*

Praise of a child

A child is like a rare bird
A child is like a precious coral.
A child is precious like brass
You cannot buy a child in the market
Not for all the money in the world

The child you buy for money is a slave
We may have twenty slaves
We may have thirty labourers
Only a child brings us joy
One's child is one's child

From *Assembly Workshop* by Yoruba Children

Prayer: God is the Creator of all things and by the birth of children he gives to parents a share in the joy and work of creation.

God our Father,
Maker of all that is living,
We praise you for the wonder and joy of creation.
We thank you from our hearts
for the life of this child (name)
for a safe delivery
and for the privilege of parenthood.
Accept our thanks and praise
through Jesus Christ our Lord. Amen.

ASB

We welcome you (name)
Applause.
The leader gives the parent(s) a gift from the school for the baby.

Follow-up:
● *Make a list of things babies can/cannot do.*
● *Make a scrapbook of stories poems and pictures for the parents of the baby.*
● *Write a group poem "In praise of a child," in which each child contributes a line, perhaps beginning each with "Babies are .... "*

BAPTISM

Aim: *To introduce a Christian festival, of which the children may have had some experience, using the symbolism of light. To link a naming ceremony with belonging to a religious faith. To explore the characteristics of different times.*

Aids: *A small baptism candle.*

Presentation: On our birthdays we celebrate the day on which we were born; we use candles on our cakes to show how old we are. We are given a candle in celebration on another occasion — that of our baptism into the Family of the Church. On this day we are given our Christian names. (give examples). Usually our parents choose our names; what a difficult decision, for our names mean our whole character. All names have special meanings, e.g. Moira = beautiful, vague, Margaret = pearl, Peter = rock, Michael = guardian angel (use examples as the names of children occur).

Where do we get our names from? Some names are biblical. Can you think of any? (David, the shepherd king, Mary, Joseph, Jacob, Anne the mother of Mary, Ruth, disciples' names). Sometimes the names which we are christened with are historical; who can tell me some of these? (Henry, Joan (of Arc), Elizabeth, William). Or sometimes we are named after someone in the family, someone who is special, so that the person may be remembered in the new baby.

As we grow up, our names have a special meaning or significance for us, for 'my name is me', and we usually like or sometimes hate our names. Does anyone not like their Christian name, and prefer to be called by a nickname?

Often some names are shortened e.g Maggie for Margaret; Billy for William (use examples of children's own names). Sometimes we are given a nickname, usually created by something in our character or appearance (examples from children).

If we are baptised we are given our chosen Christian name and welcomed into God's family. Our parents and godparents (unless we are baptised as older children) are asked to make special promises for us, until we are old enough to make these for ourselves at confirmation — that they believe in God and Jesus Christ, and renounce evil; and that the children will be brought up in a Christian family, will learn about Jesus and will try their best to follow him.

After the priest or minister signs the baby with the cross and gives him or her the name, the parent of godparent is given a baptismal candle, like this (show the candle alight). This has been lit from the Easter Paschal candle, which symbolises God's presence. Then the priest or minister asks that the child, having passed from darkness to light by baptism, may "shine as a light in the world, to the glory of God the Father." So baptism gives us our Chirstian name and welcomes us into the Christian family in which we hope to grow.

Story: Simon and Mary were very excited. It was Sunday morning, and their baby sister, Anna was coming to church with them for the very first time today. It was going to be Anna's baptism, her special day when she was to be welcomed into the church family, and given her Christian name.

"Oh, Anna does look pretty in her long white christening dress," said Mary. "I hope she isn't going to scream," said Simon as he made a funny face at his little sister. Anna gurgled up at him and showed her first tooth. "All my pals are coming." said Simon, for today the Junior Church were going to come and share in Anna's baptism.

Soon Mr and Mrs Peters were ready. Uncle Dick, Aunt Jane and Granny, who were to be Anna's godparents were going to meet them at the Church. "Right, all ready then?" asked Dad. "Don't forget Anna's cuddly," said Mary as she ran to get ted out of the pram. At last they were all in the car and driving towards St Stephen's Church — "named after Stephen the first Christian martyr" as Simon proudly announced.

The church was full with friends and relations, as well as the usual Sunday morning congregation, and mother settled Anna down in her long white shawl, clutching 'cuddly Ted'. The children joined in the hymns and listened to the readings, and then came the special moment. Uncle Dick, Aunt Jane, Granny, Mum and Dad, the two children, and of course baby Anna, asleep in mother's arms, (much to Simon's relief!) went with the vicar and server to stand around the font, where the Easter candle, still quite tall, was burning brightly. Mary remembered that the Easter candle meant that Jesus had risen from the dead, and that he was always with them. Jesus was the beginning and the end, the Light of the World, Miss Drew had told them at Junior Church at Eastertime.

Simon and Mary listened carefully as the vicar, Mr Field, asked the godparents to make their promises. Then he took Anna in his arms and made the sign of the cross on her forehead, and, sprinkling water from the font over her head, said, "Anna, Elizabeth, I baptise you in the name of the Father, and of the Son, and of the holy Spirit." "Anna, after Granny," thought Mary. "Anna, Annie, I can call her Annie-get-your-gun when she gets older," thought Simon mischievously. Just then, Anna, feeling the splash of the water, woke up and began to cry. "Oh dear, now she's going to start screaming I suppose," thought Simon, shifting nervously on his feet as he felt all his friends grinning. "Don't worry if she cries," said Mr Field as he gently gave her back to mother.

Then the server gave Dad a small lighted candle, which was to show that by her baptism Anna had passed from darkness into light, and that she was to "shine as a light in the world to the glory of the Father."

Anna watched the flickering light and started gurgling again. All the people started clapping and Mum carried Anna around the church so that everyone could see her. The children joined in with the rest of the service and went up to the altar rail with their family for the Communion. They and Anna were given a blessing by the priest. They would share the bread and the wine with the rest of the church family when they were older and confirmed.

After the service, lots of people came to look at Anna, who, tired out by all the excitement, had fallen fast asleep. Uncle Dick took some photographs, and soon the family were on their way home. Home to a very special Sunday lunch, for it was a very special day for Anna. She had many cards and some presents, but for the moment she was gurgling happily as Mum was feeding her with her bottle.

Eating his turkey and roast potatoes, Simon watched Anna's special candle burning brightly on the table: "Hmm," he thought, as he looked at Anna's round happy face, "we'll call her anniseed ball as well!"

Prayer: Thank you God for all our names, those special nicknames used by friends and family, and our Christian names (give examples) which have been especially chosen for us, and by which we belong together in your family.

Thank you too for the gift of baptism, that through your love we may become your children. Help us always to try to keep our promises and to grow into useful and loving members of your great Family. Amen.

Follow-up:
● *Find out the meanings of your family's names. Christian and surnames. Make a favourite name poll.*
● *Make string names or a collage out of all the group's names, or learn to write names in Braille or semaphore.*
● *Older children might like to discuss whether babies should be baptised or whether the ceremony should wait until children are old enough to decide for themselves, as some Christian denominations do. Perhaps a Baptist would come in to help with the latter point of view.*

ADVENT

A Candle in the Darkness

Aim: *Through the Advent theme of Light to explore some of the symbolic associations of light over darkness, light as protection and light as showing the way to God, lights for celebration; all pointing towards the preparation for and the birth of Christ, as celebrated at Christmas.*

Aids: *One or two children with lighted candles and torches.*

Background: *Advent is a time of preparation for the coming of Christ. One of the ways in which we can prepare for Christmas is by thinking and looking at the ways in which we behave, and of how we can become more like Jesus, to be more like the candles, showing others the pathway to him.*

Presentation: A lit hall is suddenly plunged into darkness. What happens when there is a power cut at home, when all the lights go out? Children with lighted candles and torches put them on. We light candles and torches to light us on our way, to be a pathway.

What other lights show the way? Street lights, pilot lights, lighthouse lamps. Light, and especially a candle, is a sign of hope, of showing us the way to Jesus as he is born for us at Christmastime, for Jesus himself said I am the Light of the World (John 8:v.12).

Story: *Our story is of a girl who used candles to show men who were prisoners for their Christian faith the way to escape.*

St Lucia

This story comes from the fourth century when Lucia, a young Christian girl in Rome, heard of Christians hiding in the underground passages of the hills to escape persecution from the Emperor Diocletian. The Emperor was a harsh man who enjoyed killing the Christians and forcing them into the games ring with lions and bears. Lucia felt very sorry for her friends and wanted to help them. But what could she, a young girl, do? She thought for a long while and her mind went back to those dark and cold underground passages. Of course! She had often played in these passages many times when she was a child. She could take them some food and warm clothes. She would have to be careful though, for there were rivers running through the passages making them extremely slippery; indeed, if she fell into one of the fast flowing currents, she would drown. But Lucia was a brave girl and knew that this was one way in which she could serve God by using her knowledge to take food to these starving men. But wait, the passages were also very dark, how would she be able to see, for she would need her hands to carry food and to feel her way along.

Lucia was walking along in the woods as she was making these plans and saw the stars shining brightly onto the trees. This gave her an idea of how she could see in the dark underground passages: she would need lights — candles fixed to a crown of twigs that she could wear on her head. Then her hands would be free to help her on her way.

Lucia carefully gathered together everything she would need for her adventure: food, a warm cloak, a few old clothes, candles, and some strong leafy twigs which she could twist into a crown. Late that night she crept silently from the house and over the stone path leading to the entrance of a hillside passage. Now was the time to light the candles. As she struck a light, something stirred and rushed from the bushes, spitting as it went, a wild cat, one of the pack which roamed the hills hereabouts. Having recovered from her fright, Lucia tried again. Success. Placing the crown of light upon her head, she felt her way along the dark and clammy passage, which got darker and wetter as it went deeper into the hillside. Often squeaking bats flew around her head, and the ground was very slippery. Lucia groped for the walls to stop herself from slipping. Soon she heard the noise of running water so she knew that she must be getting nearer to the hideout.

She called out, "Christians, my name is Lucia. I am a friend; I have brought you some food and clothes." Suddenly, a torch appeared, held by a shivering man clothed in rags. "I am Gaius," he said. "There are many of us here, and you are most welcome. Come, join us in sharing the feast that you have brought." Lucia followed Gaius deeper into the cavern and was soon sitting with a group of men, all clothed in rags, and warming themselves by a smouldering fire. As they ate and drank, Lucia learnt of the many hardships they had endured, never being able to show their faces for fear of being arrested. Sometime later, Gaius escorted her back to the cave entrance and Lucia crept quietly home, her deed safely done, or so she thought.

The Christians survived to escape to safer lands, but a few days later Lucia was arrested by the Emperor's men. She was charged with collaborating with the outlawed Christians and was executed for her brave deed. St Lucia was one of the earliest Christian martyrs and her day is always celebrated on December 13 when children in Sweden celebrate St Lucia's day. Early in the morning, the youngest daughter in the family rises early and puts on a long white dress, with a red sash. On her head she wears a crown of leaves with candles and a star carefully fixed in the branches. She carries a plate of special St Lucia cakes and coffee, and offers them to her parents. Her brothers will also dress up in long white shirts and pointed hats, to be star boys.

Prayer:
> "I am the Light of the world" you said, Jesus.
> Light is good.
> We can see our way in the light.
> Lighten our way Lord Jesus.
>
> From *Prayers for 8–11's*

Follow-up:
- *Make a survey of as many different kinds of light as possible.*
- *Make an Advent wreath.*
- *Do some simple light experiments (Ladybird books can help).*

CHANUKKAH

Aim: *To help the children appreciate the festival of another faith, which uses the symbolism of light.*

Aids: *A model or picture of a menorah, the nine-branched candlestick used especially at this festival.*

Background: *Chanukkah is the Jewish festival of lights. Held in December, it commemorates the rededication of the temple in Jerusalem after it had been liberated from the foreign power of Antiochus IV in 165 BC. When Emperor Antiochus of Syria was ruler over Jerusalem, he decreed that pagan worship should rule the country, so the Temple of God was desecrated, everything removed and statues of pagan Greek gods set up instead. The Jews were forbidden to observe the Sabbath, or their holy days, to to read the Old Testament scriptures. After some time, a revolt was inspired by an old priest called Mattathias, he died in battle and the struggle was continued by Judah the Maccabee. After a three-year battle, the Syrians were overthrown and the temple rededicated to Jewish worship. On entering the temple, the Jews found just enough oil to light a menorah candle for one night, but miraculously, the oil lasted for eight days. This is why the festival of Chanukkah lasts for eight days. In modern times, every place of worship and home would have a menorah (show model or picture), and one branch or candle is lit each evening from the central branch, until all of the branches or candles are alight. The menorah is then placed in widows to publicise the miracle, and to remind all who passed of God's miracles throughout the ages.*

During the festival Psalms 113–118 are recited at a daily morning service; there are many parties; people wear new clothes and eat Latkes, or special potato cakes. The children are given money and presents, and often play a special game called Dieidle, with a spinning top. Games of chance are also played and there is much general feasting and thanksgiving.

Presentation: Just imagine, if you had lost something very precious to you, that someone else had scraped and scratched it, but then you were able to get it back again. This is what happened to the Jewish people long ago. Foreigners, the Syrians, had taken over their temple and put statues of pagan gods in it. This was dreadful for the Jews, because one of their laws was that people must not try to make pictures or statues of God, because he was too great, too wonderful to be imagined by the human mind.

After fighting that lasted for three years, the Jews, led by a great warrior, Judah the Maccabee, recaptured the temple and rededicated it to God. When Judah entered the temple, he wanted to light the special lamp that burned as a sign that this was a holy place. But there was only enough oil to burn for one day. Amazingly, the oil lasted for eight whole days.

The feast of Chanukkah lasts for eight days to celebrate this great achievement. Each day, in every Jewish home, a *menorah,* or candle-holder for nine candles is the focus of attention. From the candle in the middle, one candle is lit the first night, two the second, until on the eighth evening, all eight candles are lighted.

Many celebrations mark this time: children receive gifts each day, everyone wears new clothes, and there is special food, such as Latkes, (potato cake).

The festival of Chanukkah, like Christmas, comes in December, when the days are very short, and the lighted *menorah* is placed in the window to remind everyone passing by that this is a special season.

Prayer: Dear Lord God, we rejoice with all Jewish people everywhere at this festival of Chanukkah. We thank you Lord, that we can worship you freely in churches and synagogues in our country today. Your gift of light is very special Lord: when we see candles and lamps burning it makes us feel that you are very near. Thank you Lord. Amen.

Follow-up

● *Make a* menorah *collage, and in the middle of each candle flame make a picture of different activities during the Chanukkah celebrations; new clothes, presents, food, dancing, special games, the temple and synagogue.*

● *Make Latkes — Jewish potato cakes eaten at Chanukkah. Grate four potatoes, drain well, then mix with a grated onion, four tablespoons of S R flour, two eggs, salt and pepper. Fry tablespoons of the mixture in 1cm of oil in a heavy frying pan until brown on both sides. Serve piping hot.*

DIWALI

Aim: *Celebrating festivals of light in other faiths — to seek a common theme and to learn a little of other traditions in order to establish an understanding and tolerance of other people and their beliefs and practices.*

Background: *Other religions also have festivals of Light. Diwali is the Hindu festival of light, held in the Hindu month of Karttika (October/November). Diwali means 'a row of lights' and marks the new year — Lakshmi puja, when oil lamps are left burning on a window sill in most Hindu homes as a welcome to the goddess Lakshmi, to bring good fortune. At this time people wear new clothes and give presents and sweets.*

Presentation:

The Story of Rama and Sita

Many hundreds of years ago, in the kingdom of Ayodhaya (Au-yoh-dja), lived a wise and good king called Dasaratha. He had three sons, Rama, Bharata, and Laksharma, and as he grew older he decided to pass the kingdom to Rama, his favourite. When Dasaratha told his subjects that Rama was to be their new king, everyone was very happy. Everyone, that is, except for his third wife Queen Kaikeyi. She was furious, for she wanted her son, Bharata to be king. She was so cross that she went to the king and reminded him of a promise he had made to her many years before, when she had saved the king's life during a fierce battle: "You made me a solemn promise, O King," she said, "and now you must grant me two things. First, you must make Bharata your king instead of Rama, and secondly you must send Rama and his wife Sita away into the forest for fourteen years." Dasaratha was very upset indeed, but he knew that he would have to do as his queen wished, so he sent for Rama and told him of the queen's wishes. Rama tried to comfort his sad father, and promised that after the fourteen

100

years he would return to the kingdom. Laksharma too was angry at the queen's plan, and decided that he would join Rama and Sita in their life in the forest. So together they packed their things and sadly said farewell to the King.

During this time Bharata had been away visiting his grandfather. When he returned and saw the people weeping and heard of the queen's plan, he too was very angry and told her that he would never be king, for it was Rama's rightful inheritance. Bharata went and searched deep in the forest, and after much travelling he found Rama and Sita living happily amongst fruit trees and tamed wild animals, who had grown to love him and the gentle Sita.

Bharata begged Rama to return to claim his throne, but Rama refused saying that he must carry out his father's promise to his mother, so Bharata sadly returned home. Whilst living in the forest, Rama, Sita and Laksharmi had many adventures, for wild demons often roamed around them and tormented the people and animals. Rama and Laksharmi fought many long battles to overcome them. The chief of these was Ravana, king of the island of Lamka. He loved beautiful women, and, having heard that Sita was living in the forest, he plotted to capture her and make her his wife. Ravana had magical powers, and one day he turned into a beautiful golden deer, which Sita wished to have as a pet. Rama followed the deer deep into the forest and, when he shot it with his bow, the animal cried out in Rama's own voice. Rama was amazed and realised that this was a trick of Ravana's and that he had left Sita alone and unguarded at home.

Far away in the hut, Sita saw an old crippled man calling out for help, and, kindhearted as she was, she rushed out to help him. Immediately the old man vanished, and in his place was Ravana, the wicked ten-headed king of the demons. He seized Sita and carried her off to his chariot in the trees, and away they flew across the seas to the island of Lanka.

Rama and Laksharmi hurried home, only to find that Sita had been kidnapped. "Come Rama," said Laksharmi, "we must hurry and search for her." They travelled for days and months, but saw no trace of the lovely Sita. Then one day, they met a tribe of monkey people and their leader Hanuman, with whose help they learnt that Sita was being held a prisoner by Ravana on the island of Lanka. But Lanka was such a long way from India, how oculd they reach her in time? Hanuman had an idea: "I shall go," he said, and with one giant leap, he flew into the air, over the sea and landed on the island. After a long search he found Sita closely guarded by demons, but seizing his opportunity Hanuman threw a ring to her. The ring belonged to Rama so Sita knew that he was near and trying to save her.

Rama and his monkey friends were busy making a bridge of boulders all the way across the sea to Lanka, and when the demons attempted to cross over there was a tremendous battle. Rama, Laksharmi and the monkeys all fought bravely against the magic of the demons and overcame their evil powers. Soon Rama and Sita were joyfully reunited.

As the fourteen years of Rama's exile were now over, they were able to return to Ayodhya, and as they approached the city in a flying chariot, they were greeted by a mass of bright lights. All the people had put lamps in their windows to light them on their way, and to welcome them home.

Bharata was overjoyed to see his brother again and started making preparations for Rama's coronation. When Rama was crowned the rightful king of Ayodhya, everyone was happy once more.

Prayer: As we prepare for Christmas, we remember before you O Lord, the Hindu people as they celebrate Diwali, welcoming again their great king, Rama. We praise you for the gift of light, light which showed Rama the way home, and all lights which are signposts to pathways in our own country. May we always take care of your gifts. Amen.

Follow-up:
- *Dramatise the story, making masks for the characters.*
- *Make* diva, *boat-shaped candleholders, from clay or salt dough. After forming the shape, with a firm base, hollow the middle; place a little oil in it, and make a cotton string wick to light.*

CHRISTMAS CUSTOMS

Aim: *These particular customs have been chosen to continue the theme of light which has been explored during Advent. It is hoped that children will be encouraged to look at familiar Christmas symbols and discover their origins, and their Christian symbolism which is still alive for us today.*

Aids: *A star, candles and either a school Christmas tree or a small tree.*

Presentation: The bright star of Bethlehem leads us to the cradle of Jesus; an astronomical guide leads all to the one who was to become the Light of the world. Many Old Testament prophecies foretold that the birth of Jesus would be shown by a new, bright star, and many people were waiting for this to happen. (The star is put on top of the tree.)

Candles too symbolise Jesus: the wax represents his body, the wick, his soul, and the flame, his divine nature. A candle is a sign of welcome; in Ireland, candles are lit on Christmas Eve and are left shining all night in a window. The door too is often left open, symbolically to welcome the Holy Family in case they are seeking shelter.

We often put candles on a Christmas tree. This first arose as a pagan custom. The Romans during the feast of Saturnalia fastened candles to trees in an effort to ask the sun to return to the earth. (It was believed that the sun died during the winter.) When Christianity became the religion of the country candles were given their Christian symbolism. Spruce trees are often chosen as Christmas trees because their roots are in the earth, and they point towards heaven. It is thought that during the middle ages it was Martin Luther who first put candles on a Christmas tree, in an attempt to show his family how beautiful the starlight sky must have been above the stately fir trees on the night that Jesus was born. Many more legends surround the fir tree:

The Christ Child and the Woodman

One cold Christmas Eve, long long ago, a woodman and his family were sitting round their blazing log fire when suddenly there was a knock on the door of their cottage. Wondering who on earth would be calling on them so late and in such snowy weather, the woodman went to see who it was.

Standing outside was a little child. He was shivering with cold, and he looked hungry and tired out. The astonished woodman led the child inside.

'Who can he be? Why is he alone in the forest?' exclaimed the woodman's wife.

At once she set her children to rubbing back life into the boy's poor frozen limbs, while she busied herself in making him some hot milk to drink.

'He can sleep in my bed tonight,' said the eldest son. 'I will sleep on the floor.' So the exhausted child was put into a warm bed and he fell asleep at once.

In the morning, the woodman's family was awakened by the sound of beautiful voices singing.

'It is like the sound of angels,' they whispered.

Suddenly the room was filled with light. When they looked at the child they had sheltered, they realised that it was the Christ Child himself.

The woodman and his family fell to their knees in awe, but the Christ Child went outside to a small fir tree and touched its branches. At once the tree shone with a great light.

'You took me into your home,' said the Christ Child, 'You gave me the gifts of food, shelter, warmth, and kindness. Now here is my gift to you — a tree that will remind you at Christmas time that you took me into your hearts. May it shine to show my love for you, and may it bear gifts as a token of your love for one another.'

Christmas trees became a German custom, and it was not until the reign of Queen Victoria that Christmas trees were brought to England by Prince Albert. He brought the first Christmas tree to Windsor Castle in 1841. Ever since 1947, the people of Oslo in Norway have given a gift of a Christmas tree to the City of London, as an expression of gratitude for British help during World War II. You can see it every year in Trafalgar Square.

Let us put our candles on our Christmas tree and remember their meaning for us as we celebrate this Christmas (a few children light the candles).

Poem:
> Light the candles on the tree,
> Christ was born for you and me.
> Light the candles in the hall,
> He was born to help us all.
> Light the candles up and down,
> In the country and the town.
> Light the candles everywhere,
> He was born a baby fair.

> C. Rossetti

Put the room into darkness and spend a few moments silence looking at the flickering candles on the tree.

Prayer:
> Lord,
> let us
> be your candles,
> each and
> every day.   Amen.

Follow-up:
- *Make your own candles.*
- *Find out about other Christmas customs, or Christmas in other lands.*
- *Make a survey of family customs within the group.*

WHAT CAN I GIVE?

Aim: *To help children to become aware that Christmas is not always a happy time for all people. To help to respond to God's gift of his Son to us, by giving something in return, specifically to the underprivileged. "Crisis at Christmas" is one example of just such an activity.*

Background: *Crisis at Christmas is an organisation set up to help the lonely and homeless of London to have an enjoyable Christmas. It is run mostly by volunteers with a small back-up team. Each year they take over a building in London and convert it to an Open House for the Christmas period, usually from December 23rd until early in January. Fund raising for this time, for it needs a great deal of money, care and organisation for such a successful venture, includes a carol festival at Southwark Cathedral, and a sixty-mile sponsored walk, from Canterbury to London. Large food stores give food; many other organisations throughout the country donate money, or clothing. Catering students often do most of the cooking and food is stored until it is needed. Doctors and First Aiders give their time and skills as do about four hundred volunteers who are needed to help over the Open Christmas.*

Presentation: What do you like best about Christmas? Giving and receiving presents? Decorations? The Christmas story? Special food? (Ask the children for ideas.) All these things can help us to be happy on this special day; but Christmas day is not always a happy day for everyone. Can you think of any people for whom this might be so? (Ask for children's ideas.) Some are people in hospital, broken families, the very poor and the lonely.

Many people are living rough in London, finding shelter in tunnels, and derelict houses; and Christmas is often not a happy time for them. Crisis at Christmas is an organisation which tries to help such people as these at Christmas time by taking over a large building in London and providing an Open

Christmas: room to sleep, daily meals, including a fine Christmas dinner, a change of clothes, entertainment, and a daily surgery, where anyone can see a doctor. No one is ever turned away and the only rule is that people must leave their bottles outside (many are alcoholics). Lots of different people come to the Open Christmas. Last year there was Lisa who had arrived from Liverpool earlier in the year. She had found casual work during the summer, working in cafes, and selling souvenirs which provided enough money to pay for a hostel bed. When the visitors went, so did her job; so Lisa had been living rough. Not wanting to return to her mother in Liverpool, she had come to the Open Christmas. Some people came back year after year: there was Billy who had spent many Christmases at the Open, usually turning up icy cold, underfed and drunk, but always with a present and card for the cook. This year, he arrived with his present and card as usual, but bright-eyed, and sober, and smartly dressed: "I just had to come and tell you I'm alright," he said. "I've found a room and I'm settled. But I'll never forget my good friends at Crisis." That was Christmas present enough for anyone.

So being with family and friends at Christmas is just as important or more so than all the presents and entertainment, for these lonely people and for all of us. And we give thanks to God for the birth of his Son into a human family where he could receive just such loving care.

Prayer: What can I give him,
Poor as I am.
If I were a shepherd,
I could bring a lamb.
If I were a wise man,
I would do my part;
Yet what can I give him,
Give my heart.

C. Rossetti

Follow-up:
- *Plan a Christmas giving project: a party for the elderly, a collection of toys for a children's home or the Salvation Army, a carol concert for Crisis at Christmas.*
- *Ask the children to write a Christmas message to their village, town or city, or to the whole world.*

COMMUNITY

Aim: *To explore the idea of what a community is and how it can contribute to our lives.*

Aids: *A piece of cake and a glass of squash. A large sign reading COMMUNITY.*

Presentation: If I said the word "community", what would come into your minds? Perhaps you would think of your village shops and hall; perhaps you would think of your city neighbourhood, with a playground, and sports centre. People sometimes like to be alone, but more often they want to be with other people, and a community is a group of people, usually between two and three thousand, who live, work and play together.

When people live in one place, but work far away in another town, it is difficult for them to feel at home in their community because they are away from it most of the time. When people move from one community to another, it takes a time to meet new friends and feel part of their new neighbourhood. When people move very often, they get more and more isolated, and unhappy. They are far from their families and their friends.

We all need to feel that we belong, that we can recognise familiar faces in the shops, that we can join in local clubs and churches, that we will find friends to play with in the recreation field.

Long ago, groups of families used to live in the same place sometimes for hundreds of years, and everyone helped out if there was illness, or if someone was injured, because everyone knew everybody else so well, that one missing face was immediately noticed.

Today, however, you might live in a large block of flats without any garden, so you might never meet your neighbours at all. New faces would appear all the time, and you would not know where they have come from or if they could be trusted. How, then, can we build a community in today's fast moving world?

I'd like to tell you about a very special community centre right in the middle of London. It doesn't have any sign outside to say that it's a community centre, but everyone who walks through the door is greeted by name. Harry's corner store has been there, looked after by Harry and his mother for over twenty-five years. He sells newspapers, sweets, groceries, cards and gifts and creates a lot of good will.

Harry wasn't always a shopkeeper. He travelled all over the world, worked in a publishing firm and lived in America for a time. But eventually he came back to the shop. "It's people," he explained. "I just love them. They come in and tell me their troubles. They come in just to show me their new babies. They come in for a bit of chat when they're lonely.

"One day, an old lady hobbled through the door, Doris her name was. She'd just had an operation for arthritis and had to use crutches for some months. She was dreadfully afraid of falling, and the social services had offered her a bleeper, to call a friend if she fell. Trouble was, all her friends had either died or moved and she didn't know anyone well enough to ask to be her call person.

"Well, I knew Doris, and I said, 'Luv, just give me your bleeper. I'm around all day every day. You know I'll hear you.' The look on her face, just pure relief. And here it is under the counter, just in case."

Harry not only gives out good will. He also helps people to meet, introduces his customers to each other. Recently, he even threw a party — an all-day party for the whole community to celebrate the twenty-fifth anniversary of his shop. Harry invited every customer who came into the shop for weeks beforehand, and they all came, from ninety-year old Doris to the newest baby, with her mum of course.

Harry put out a comfortable chair for his mother, and served up cake and drinks from ten in the morning until ten at night. That little corner store was packed with people coming and going the whole day. They talked and sang; they told stories about the neighbourhood. Lots of people met others who lived near them but they'd never known, and so new friendships were formed.

As the last glass was raised, Harry's customers toasted him and said, "Here's to the next twenty-five year's of Harry's Corner Store!" There's no doubt that, as long as Harry's there, those streets and blocks of flats will continue to be a real community.

Prayer: Dear God, bless our communities. May they be happy and welcoming places. Help us to respect the property of others, to keep our streets free of rubbish, and our playgrounds clean for all to enjoy. We thank you for shopkeepers like Harry who make their customers their friends. May we be willing to listen to our neighbours, so that we live happily together. Amen.

Follow-up:

- *Make a large map of your neighbourhood/village and glue on painted pictures of where people meet: shops, the school, the church, the community hall, the playing fields.*
- *Discuss how a sense of community might be built up in your area. What project might involve people of all ages?*

SERVICE

Aim: *To show that to build a sense of community, everyone must contribute as well as receive benefits.*

Aids: *A shopping bag, a pet food dish.*

Presentation: Just by the school in the village of Down Fenwick, there was a new block of flats for elderly people. One of the tenants, a widow living on her own, used to sit by the window each morning and watch the children on their way to school. The window was on the ground floor, and Boots, her black and white cat, used to leap down on fine days, and let the children pat him. One or two of the girls used to carry him up to the school gate and he would purr all the way, pleased at the extra attention. Then he would stroll back to the garden underneath the window and wait for the next pat and cuddle.

The children knew his name was Boots because they sometimes heard the lady call him in for his breakfast. She always had a cheery wave for the children, but they didn't know her name. She was just The-lady-in-the-Window.

One Monday morning, the lady was not in the window, and there was no sign of Boots. "Perhaps she's gone on holiday," said Samantha. All that week, there was no sign of anyone in the flat, and the geraniums were beginning to wilt. The children asked their teacher, Mr Fletcher, if he could find out what had happened to the lady and Boots.

After school, Mr Fletcher stopped by the flats and rang the lady's bell. Mrs Willow, the nameplate above the bell said. No answer. Then he rang the next-door neighbour's bell. When a man opened the door, Mr Fletcher asked him if he knew what had happened to the lady. "Sad that," he replied. "Sunday, she was crossing the road and a scooter came into her, broke her ankle and bad bruises all over. She's still in hospital would be my guess."

"And her cat Boots?" enquired Mr Fletcher.

"Oh, the social services put it into a cattery," replied the

112

man.

Next day, when Mr Fletcher told his class what he had found out, they were quick to respond. "Let's send her a card and some flowers," suggested Mark. They all drew pictures of Boots and the lady in the window with her geraniums, and sent them off with a large bunch of roses to Mrs Willow care of the local hospital.

The next Monday, after school, some of the children saw an ambulance outside the flats. They rushed round to see who was in it, and there was Mrs Willow being wheeled down a ramp in a wheelchair, a large plaster round her right ankle. The ambulance men had to lift her over her front step, and she waved to the children. "I'm back, you see, I have missed you all. And I've missed Boots too. But he won't be back yet, for you see I couldn't bend down to feed him."

"We're glad you're back, too," piped up Mark. "Did you get our flowers? And the pictures?"

"I did indeed. And they cheered up my stay in hospital a good deal, I can tell you. Thank you all very much."

The children reported back to Mr Fletcher that Mrs Willow had come back, but she had to stay in a wheelchair and couldn't get over the step. "And she can't have Boots back, either," said Jonathan, "because she can't bend down to feed him."

"Well," said Mr Fletcher, "we've been doing a project on our community. Shall we show how much community spirit we have and help out Mrs Willow?"

A loud chorus of "Yes!" greeted the suggestion and together, the class drew up a schedule of visits to feed Boots before school, and do messages for Mrs Willow after school. Mr Fletcher had the class write notes to all their parents explaining why they had to be early to school some days and late home other days, and then he went off to see Mrs Willow again.

She was so pleased to think that Boots could come home again, and phoned the cattery right away. Next morning, there Mrs Willow was by the open window, and Boots was in the garden eagerly awaiting the first pat of the morning. He was delighted to be free again.

A week later, a ramp appeared outside Mrs Willow's door, and she could wheel herself out. The children still had to go into the shops for her because they all had steps, but she could wait outside on the pavement and look in the windows to see what was good to buy that day.

After chatting to her, the children learned that she had four grandchildren, but they lived far away in Canada, and she'd only been able to visit them twice. The school children were very important to her, because she had once been a teacher herself, and since she had retired, she had missed being with children.

"That's why Boots is so fond of you all," she said. "He was a school cat and always loved being the centre of attention."

Do you know that over six weeks, the children missed only one visit, and that was because David caught the 'flu. But his mum sent his big sister Joanna instead, so Boots didn't miss his breakfast.

And now, Mrs Willow is back on her feet, and comes over to school now and again to have a chat with Mr Fletcher's class, her guardian angels, she calls them, and they giggle.

Prayer: Dear God, we thank you for opportunities to serve in our communities, in school, in brownies and cubs, in our churches. Make us aware of needs, and not to pass by on the other side if we can do something to help. When we help, may we do it cheerfully and responsibly, not forgetting our turn. Amen.

Follow-up:
- *Do a project on services in your community. The area nurse might be willing to come in and talk about her visiting.*
- *Discuss some of the problems of growing older: the aches and pains, the forgetfulness, the slowing down, with a view to helping the children to be sensitive to elderly people. Ask someone's grandparent in to tell how things have changed.*
- *Do a survey of your community to see how many places a wheelchair could/could not go.*

Preface to *The Cowshed*

This is a nativity play intended to be performed by a mixed group of adults and children. The only speaking part for a child is the role of David the shepherd boy. The children, however, have plenty of miming and noise-making. This is an adventurous play in modern language; it makes us look again at the antiseptic crib scenes we often produce, and shows that Jesus' birth was a human situation, with all the detail that requires.

THE COWSHED

A play for Christmas

by Rosina Elston

SCENE 1   *A street in Bethlehem*

Centre stage, an inn door. This should be obvious by the sign hanging outside. The door is used during the scene so must be hinged in order to open. An alternative could be a curtained entrance.

Characters — Souvenir Seller
Innkeeper
David, a shepherd boy
May
Joseph
Reverend professor
Martha, barmaid and midwife
Children

The souvenir seller is seated on the floor in front of the inn door. His wares are spread on the ground around him, making it impossible for anyone to enter or leave the inn without stepping over them, or on them .... The children of Bethlehem play in the street around him; marbles, singing games, conkers, etc. Above their chatter, the souvenir seller can be heard ....

Souvenir Seller: Come on! Come and buy! Genuine Bethlehem souvenirs! Look at the workmanship in these wooden bowls, made from trees which were growing when King David was alive!

Stone carvings from the pebbles which David used to kill Goliath! Shepherd's crooks like David himself had when he was only a lad in the fields! Come on! Come and buy! This is your last chance at these prices. Genuine reductions for census time!

116

The children wander over and listen, and wander away again to resume their games.

Enter David holding a crook. He is clearly looking for something. He goes to each group of children and asks them. They shrug their shoulders and carry on playing. He stands in front of the souvenir seller blocking him off from the audience.

David: Please sir, have you seen ....?

The souvenir seller pushes him to one side.

Souvenir Seller: Get out of my light, boy! I can't see anybody! How do you expect me to earn an honest living with you blocking my view?

David moves to one side, but refuses to be silenced.

David: Please sir .... have you seen a sheep? Please sir .... I've lost a sheep, well, a baby sheep. I was leading them out of the fold and a dog frightened it. I've been looking for it all day. I think it came into town .... I followed it through the gates but now it's gone .... It's only a small sheep, about this high and it sounds like this ....

He begins to imitate it. The children stop their playing and watch. The souvenir seller watches open-mouthed.

Souvenir Seller: A sheep? A sheep! You're looking for a sheep in Bethlehem today? *(He laughs)* You must be mad! How will you find one little sheep among all these people? *(He frowns)* What do you want me to do? I can't chase after a lost sheep. I've got a living to earn! Of course I haven't seen your sheep. It's probably in a stewpot by now. Go away! Go back to the rest of the flock, or they'll run away too!

David turns away and begins to ask members of the audience if they've seen a sheep. Meanwhile Mary and Joseph enter from the back of the audience. Mary is leaning heavily on Joseph. She is obviously pregnant and looks very tired. Joseph is leading a sheep on a length of string. David sees them, and the sheep, and runs to meet them.

David: My sheep! Oh, you've found my sheep! Oh sir, you've found my lamb!

Joseph gives him the sheep and David makes a fuss over the animal. The children give a big cheer.

Joseph: So he belongs to you, does he? We found him wandering along the road back there. He must have liked the look of us because he began to follow us. I put him on a rope hoping he would lead us to some shelter tonight. My wife cannot travel much farther. She is due to ....

Enter the Innkeeper through the door. He makes a great noise and kicks the souvenirs out of his way.

Innkeeper: Get out! How dare you! Get out of my way! How dare you put your rubbish outside my front door! Who gave you permission to use my pavement for your cheating trickery? I'll have the police on you!

The souvenir seller scrambles after his goods, retrieving what he can. Some of the children help him while others make faces at the innkeeper when he's looking elsewhere. The innkeeper addresses the audience ....

I would like to make it clear to all of you that this is a First Class Hotel. When you stay here you get five star treatment. Only the best is good enough for us .... for good money of course!

He points to the children and the souvenir seller

No one would believe it if they saw the riff raff that hangs around here. Go away all of you. Have you nothing better to do?

No one moves and some of the children make more faces — without him seeing of course.

Didn't you hear what I said? I don't want you upsetting my guests with your noise and ....

Joseph steps forward to speak to him, and the innkeeper notices the sheep next to him.

What's that? A Sheep?! What's a sheep doing here? A nasty, smelly, noisy sheep! If you don't take it away at once, I'll get the cook to put it in the pot!

David hurriedly draws the sheep further back out of reach. Joseph attracts the innkeeper's attention.

Joseph: Peace be with you, sir. Do you have any rooms to let? My wife and I have come a long way, and she is due to ....

Innkeeper: *(interrupts him rudely)* We deal only with the Best People. This is a High Class Hotel.

Joseph: *(angrily)* My family belongs to this city! I am descended from King David himself! I have come back now to be counted in the Roman census.

Innkeeper: *(interrupting again)* What is your profession? You smell of sheep. You're not a shepherd are you? Shepherds should stay in the hills. We want no shepherds here!

Joseph: You say that? You say that when the great King David himself was a shepherd here? Do you despise shepherds in

David's own city? You might as well despise King David himself! Be careful! You might even despise the great promised son of David, the Messiah, who will be God's own King for our people!

Mary puts out a hand and touches his arm. He quietens down.

I will say no more about this now. But I will tell you that I do have a 'respectable' profession. I am a builder. Ask anyone from Nazareth in Galilee and they will tell you about Joseph, the builder.

Innkeeper: *(sullenly)* What can you afford to pay? That is more to the point.

Joseph: *(angry again)* If it were not for my wife, I would rather spend the night on the hill-side with the shepherds. They know how to give hospitality!

The sound of a drum offstage stops the conversation. Enter three servants dressed in uniform. One beats a drum as the others push the children out of the way.

Servants: Out of the way! Stand back! Make way for the Reverend Professor, ben Eleazar of Bethphage!

Ben Eleazar enters. He is wearing the garb of a scholar and is accompanied by a little boy carrying a great pile of heavy books. When ben Eleazar stops in front of the inn door, he puts down the books with a great sigh of relief.

Eleazar: Where is the manager of this hotel? I wish to speak to him.

Innkeeper: *(bowing, scraping, boot-licking)* Peace be upon you, Reverend Father. I am the manager of this most honoured establishment. I and my staff are at your service.

Eleazar: *(after scrutinising the innkeeper carefully)* I need to stay in Bethlehem for the night. I have been told that this is the Best Hotel in the city. Is that true?

Innkeeper: Yes sir. Everything here is the best of the best. Once you enter these four walls you leave the dirt of the street behind you.

He indicates the watching crowd and the audience.

Eleazar: That may be so, but there is hidden dirt which is just as contaminating. Do you order your establishment according to the traditions of our fathers? Is the food prepared in the correct way? Are your staff free of ritual uncleanness? Are Gentiles and other unclean persons kept outside the gates?

Innkeeper: *(bowing a 'yes' to each of these questions)* I am proud to say, Reverend Sir, that I can answer Yes to each of these questions. I myself supervise the preparation of the food. It is inspected regularly by the teachers of the Law. Gentiles and unclean people never enter the building. We have room only for the Best.

Eleazar: Good. I will stay here. Reserve me four rooms. I must have room to study the sacred scriptures in silence. This Edict of Rome is most inconvenient. I cannot allow it to interrupt my studies.

The innkeeper bows and ushers in Eleazar and the servants. The little boy picks up the books with a sigh and follows. As the innkeeper turns to go, last of all, Joseph interrupts him.

Joseph: Please! What about us? We are desperate. Only one little room for my wife to ....

Innkeeper: Sorry! No room!

Joseph offers him money which he refuses.

Anyway, you smell of sheep. Take your woman and be off!

Mary groans and clutches her abdomen. She almost falls into Joseph's arms. Everyone seems to notice her for the first time.

Joseph: Shame on you! Would you turn us away now my wife's first child is coming?

All the children and the souvenir seller boo loudly.

Innkeeper: *(unsure now)* You never told me that! You shouldn't have brought her out in that condition ....

Joseph: Her child is on its way now, this very night! Are you going to turn her away to give birth in the street like a cow or donkey?

More booing and cries of Shame!

Innkeeper: No, no, of course not.

He shouts through the door.

Martha!

Enter Martha, the barmaid, running and worried.

Martha: Yes sir? You wanted something sir?

Innkeeper: Have you ever delivered a baby?

Martha: *(looking with sympathy at Mary)* Yes sir. I've had two of my own, and helped my sister with hers.

Innkeeper: Good! Take this woman behind the hotel to the cowshed ....

Everyone: *(shouting)* COWSHED ! ! !

Innkeeper: *(nervously)* Make her a bed with clean straw. I cannot have a baby delivered at the hotel now the Reverend Father has arrived. A woman in that condition is unclean for at least six weeks afterwards. He would leave us if he thought we'd made part of the hotel into a labour ward ....

Martha stares at him unbelieving. The children hiss softly in disapproval ....

well woman? What are you staring for? From the look of her there's not much time to lose!

Martha takes Mary from Joseph and leads her out. She shakes her head at Joseph, not allowing him to follow. The innkeeper goes back into the inn. Lights dim. Children and all except Joseph and David exit.

Joseph: What is it, lad?

David: A cowshed? You'll let your first child be born in a cowshed? My mother would look after you better than the manager of that hotel! Four rooms for one teacher. A cowshed for your wife and her first born.

Joseph: I did not choose where this child should be born, lad. Everything to do with him is in the hands of Almighty God. His ways are not our ways. If a cowshed is the birthplace of a son of David, then a cowshed can become the home of God.

David: A cowshed the home of God? What do you mean?

Joseph: I'm talking in riddles, lad. One day you'll understand. Now go back home with your sheep. He's lucky to have such a caring young shepherd. May the Almighty God care for you as you care for that sheep.

David exits.

The people who walked in darkness have seen a great light,
A light has shone upon those who live in deepest shadow.
For a child has been born to us, a son has been given to us,
And government is laid on his shoulders.
This is his name ....
    Wonderful Counsellor
      Mighty God
        Eternal Father
          Prince of Peace
His kingdom is vast, of a never-ending peace
He establishes the royal throne of David by Justice and Righteousness
From this night onwards, for evermore, the zeal of the Lord of the armies of Heaven is doing all these things.

Fade out.

SCENE 2   *A Hillside at night.*

Characters — John, Rueben, Simon (shepherds)
                Angel
                Heavenly Choir
                David

There is scope in this scene for music by the choir and, if practised, a 'glory' song by the congregation. The angel does not have to 'appear' in the conventional sense. A bright light beamed upon mirrors could produce the desired dazzling effect.

The shepherds, dressed shabbily in warm clothes, are playing cards.

John: *(yawning)* It's getting very late now. Where has that boy got to? The city at night is no place for a youngster like him.

Rueben: I do hope he's come to no harm. Strong boys like him fetch a high price in the slave market. You know how full of strangers Bethlehem is. It would be an easy thing to kidnap a boy and hide him away ....

Simon: Stop worrying, the two of you. David's a good lad. The Lord protects his own.

Rueben: I can't understand why he made all that fuss over the sheep. We have plenty left. Why bother with one little lost one?

Simon: He's like the first David, our great king. He fought bears to save his sheep.

John: And lions. Imagine killing a lion with a sling! They were great those days, the days of King David. We sent all the Philistines running back to the sea. If only we could do the same now with the Romans.

Rueben: It's no good day-dreaming. That won't get us any-where.

John: The Romans carry their eagles along our roads and kick us with their leather boots. If only we could hit back ....

Rueben: We're luckier than most. We can hide in the hills and keep out of their way.

Simon: The Roman empire cannot last for ever. You have heard the old prophets about the coming of the Great King. He will be even greater than David. He will be anointed with the Spirit of the Lord God Almighty.

Rueben: You'd better be quiet about that. It's alright saying such things up here in the hills, but down in the town even the walls have ears. That's treason you're talking. Herod is our king now. You know what that means! Do you want to disappear in the middle of the night? or waste away as a galley slave .... or hang in pain on a cross, just because you whispered the word 'Messiah'?

They look at each other uneasily. Suddenly there is a Great Light. They fall back, shielding their eyes.

Angel: Do not be afraid. Listen. I am bringing you joyful news for everyone. Today, in the city of David, a Saviour has been born to you, He is the Messiah, the King who comes from God, the Lord of all. Do not be afraid. What I am saying is true. This is the sign which will show you. You will find the newborn baby wrapped in his swaddling cloth, lying in a feeding trough.

Hark the Herald — Audience.

Chorus of Praise. All the lights can come on for the audience to stand and sing. The shepherds remain dumbfounded. Lights out — Silence.

John: The Messiah! The Christ! The Saviour of Israel!

Rueben: Born in Bethlehem, the city of David!

Simon: A new baby, wrapped up warm and tight .... lying in a feeding trough?

All: In a Feeding Trough?

Enter David with the sheep. At first they do not see him. He has to push the sheep in front of them before they come round.

David: Look! I've found my sheep! I looked everywhere .... I thought I'd lost him. Then I met a man and his wife leading him with some string. He had followed them. They gave him back to me. They've come to Bethlehem for the census. But do you know what? There was no room for them at the hotel, so she had to go to the cowshed to have their baby. The manager of the hotel was so mean ....

Simon: Did you say she went to have a baby in a cowshed?

David: Yes. That's because the manager of the hotel was so mean ....

John: Where would you put a new-born baby if you were in a cowshed?

David: What?

Rueben: I should think a bed of hay just big enough to hold a baby and small enough to keep out draughts would be ....

John and Simon: .... a feeding trough.

They cheer and dance around, linking arms. David looks on, bemused.

It's true! The angels were real! They told us!

David: What's happened? What's the matter with you?

John: Lead us to that cowshed, young David. The little new-born baby is the Messiah, the Saviour of Israel!

David: Is that what the man meant when he said a cowshed could be the home of God?

Rueben: Your baby is greater than King Herod or the Roman Emperor himself!

David: More important than that teacher at the hotel?

Simon: The Power of God is with him. We have seen and heard the armies of Heaven tonight. Lead on, David. We'll tell you on the way.

They exit.

SCENE 3 *The Final Tableau*

Mary, Joseph and the Baby (in a feeding trough), centre. The shepherds enter from the back and run down to the 'cowshed'. Mary and Joseph show them the baby. They kneel and David gives Joseph the sheep. They come back into the audience and collect the children, souvenir seller, and all the characters except the innkeeper and Eleazar. These two come walking from the front to the back of the hall, oblivious to all the excitement. They exit. The characters in the play circulate among the audience with the news that 'the Saviour has been born'. Everyone eventually is kneeling. At the end the innkeeper and Eleazar re-enter slowly, fearfully, their heads hung with shame. Mary holds the baby towards them ....

Mary: Whoever welcomes a child, welcomes the Lord Jesus. Whoever welcomes the Lord Jesus, welcomes the God and Father of us all.

The innkeeper and Eleazar kneel, barehead, offering presents. Joseph then invites us all to stand and rejoice with Mary in the words of her song:

"Tell out my soul ...."

Happy Christmas!